GPS for Walkers

An introduction to gps and digital maps

Clive Thomas

JARROLD
publishing

Text:	Clive Thomas
Photography:	R. Thomas-Martinez, Clive Thomas, Elizabeth Walsh. Photograph of 'Downland landscape near Hollingbourne', p. 63, John Brooks and Jarrold Publishing
Editorial:	Ark Creative (UK) Ltd.
Design:	Ark Creative (UK) Ltd.

A CIP catalogue record for this book is available from the British Library.

Jarrold Publishing, an imprint of Pitkin Publishing Ltd

ISBN: 978-0-7117-4445-5

While every care has been taken to check the accuracy and reliability of the information in this book, the author and publisher cannot accept responsibility for errors or omissions or for changes in details given. It is advisable to act with due care and attention, and follow basic safety rules, at all times when walking in the countryside, and to observe the law and the Countryside Code.
   For more information visit the official website of the Jarrold *Pathfinder* and *Short Walks* guides: www.totalwalking.co.uk

First published 2006 by Jarrold Publishing; reprinted 2006 and 2007. Revised and reprinted 2008.

Printed in Singapore. 5/08

Pitkin Publishing Ltd
Healey House,
Dene Road,
Andover,
Hampshire
SP10 2AA

email: info@totalwalking.co.uk
www.totalwalking.co.uk

pathfinder® guide

GPS for Walkers

An introduction to gps and digital maps

Clive Thomas

JARROLD
publishing

Contents

✏ Note:

GPS in capital letters refers to the Global Positioning System: gps in lower case letters refers to the gps receiver also sometimes referred to as the 'unit' or 'receiver'. (It receives radio signals from the satellites but does not transmit any signals.)

There are quite a lot of acronyms in gps matters. They are kept to a minimum here; some of the more common ones are used, however, because they appear on your gps screens and in the literature accompanying your receiver.

Add a new dimension to navigation with a gps

Introduction

This is a book written by a walker for walkers who wish to enhance their walking experience and make it safer. Many people find a gps difficult to come to terms with and so they avoid using one. The manuals sold with gps do not necessarily provide the whole answer while the approach taken by books and experts can be too technical for the average walker. The premise of this book is that in order to drive a car you do not need to understand the workings of the internal combustion engine, fascinating though they might be. The same goes for gps. To keep things simple, one particular model is used in the descriptions, on the principle that once you can drive one car, you can drive any car. Then you can turn to your manual for details of how your particular receiver operates.

Garmin eTrex

The model used in the examples is the yellow entry-level Garmin eTrex. This compact, inexpensive receiver is readily available on the high street, offers all the functions a walker is likely to need and is straightforward to use. Also it is tried and tested. *You do not need to own this model to understand what follows. It is used to illustrate the way a gps functions.* Once you understand how to get the most out of the eTrex you can move on to other makes and models should you wish to do so.

Magellan eXplorist 210

There is a large number of gps receivers on the market to choose from and new models are being produced all the time, but all gps receivers work in essentially the same way and present the information you will need in similar terms and displays. Most gps receivers are made by US manufacturers so the manuals and language used is sometimes a little different from British usage but this should present no difficulties. The three main manufacturers of gps suitable for walkers are Garmin, Magellan and Lowrance. You will not go far wrong buying gps receivers made by any of these companies.

The GPS system is based on some very complex science and mathematics. Walkers do not need to worry about all this but a general understanding of how the system works, its advantages and limitations, and how to program your receiver are necessary to enable you to get the best out of this immensely useful and entertaining navigational aid. It is no exaggeration to say that the gps offers one of the greatest advances in navigation since the invention of the compass by the Chinese over 2,000 years ago.

Walkers should not rely on a gps as their only means of navigation. Think of your gps as complementary to your map and compass, not as a substitute.

Having considered the basic functions and use of the gps, the next part of the book examines PC programs that can be used with it. Again, the approach is non-technical and concentrates on the advantages of gps to the walker. Remember that you do not need to be computer-literate to use a gps. A PC and the Internet do open up a whole new range of possibilities. You can spend hours trawling through endless information and websites, much of it highly specialised – but this is not essential to enjoying your gps.

Discover how to use a gps at home and abroad

Some guidance is given on buying a gps, and we take a look at some aspects of navigation relevant to using your gps both at home and abroad. For example, to make full use of your gps you do need to know about map references and how, in the UK, to use a six-figure Ordnance Survey reference. You may also want to use your gps abroad and this is also considered. Having read this book you may want to explore the subject further and so we suggest a number of sources.

The Global Positioning System

The Global Positioning System consists of 24 navigational satellites plus some 'spares' (up to 32 satellites in all) and five ground stations. The satellites transmit radio signals that can be used by gps receivers to locate position anywhere above or on the planet, though not under water.

Each satellite weighs approximately 1,860 pounds, is five feet wide and 17.5 feet long. The satellites orbit the Earth every 11 hours 58 minutes at a height of 10,900 miles and rely on solar energy for power. They are built to last about ten years and so need constant replacement. Satellites send out their own unique radio signals that tell your receiver where they are. The time the radio signal takes to reach the gps enables it to compute the distance the satellites are from it and so work out its location, in all kinds of weather. Satellites are arranged in orbits so that at any one time a gps can receive radio signals from at least six satellites. Contact with four is necessary for a 3-D 'fix', i.e. location and altitude, whereas contact with three gives only a 2-D reading which does not contain any altitude information.

The system was developed by the American military (NAVSTAR) as a guidance system for targeting their cruise missiles enabling an accuracy of 1–5 metres. The military soon realised they had created a double-edged weapon which could be employed against them so they deliberately introduced a random error into the system, Selective Availability or SA, and so reduced its precision to non-American military users. SA was turned off in May 2000 at which point accuracy for commercial receivers improved from 100 metres to the present c.15 metres. When the US invaded Afghanistan after 9/11 they were able to jam the signal regionally to stop the opposition using the global positioning system against their forces. It has been claimed the Americans' rapid battlefield success in both Gulf wars was owing to their satellite system.

The GPS system is still dominated and funded by the Americans but the Europeans are planning their own satellite network and the European Space Agency (ESA) launched its first of 30 planned satellites in December 2005. The system will be fully operational by about 2011.

'Galileo will be Europe's own global navigation system providing a highly accurate, guaranteed global positioning service under civilian control. It will be inter-operable with the US Global Positioning System (GPS) and Russia's Global Navigation Satellite System (Glonass), the two other global satellite systems. Galileo will deliver real-time positioning accuracy down to the metric range with unrivalled integrity.' (ESA)

Anyone can use the satellite system. Access is completely free. When EGNOS and WAAS (see page 45) are fully operational, position accuracy will be between 3–5 metres for recreational users. Already very costly gps receivers can attain accuracies to within one centimetre. The GPS is now widely used: aircraft and ships have long navigated by it. On land its uses are expanding rapidly. Archaeologists, surveyors, map-makers, conservationists, environmental agencies, foresters, the mobile phone network, the police, the emergency services, banks, walkers, runners and motorists with their sat-nav units (GPS will also be used for road pricing) are just a few of the many users of the Global Positioning System. In Japan some children have receivers sewn into their clothing so that their parents may track their movements on the Internet. There could be important implications for blind people and Alzheimer patients who could be more easily found if they became disoriented. The potential applications of the GPS seem endless.

What information can I expect my gps to give me?

1 Location

The most valuable piece of information your receiver will give you is your location anywhere on the planet. When used in the UK this is a 10-digit map reference plus two letters (British Grid) e.g. NY 21540 07211 (unless you choose to use latitude and longitude). The more familiar 6-figure reference (e.g. 215072) used by walkers can be obtained by just dropping the last two figures in each of the two parts of the reading, giving you the co-ordinates to locate yourself on any Ordnance Survey map.

> *The most valuable piece of information your receiver will give you is your location anywhere on the planet. This is sufficient reason for owning a gps.*

This, arguably, is sufficient reason for owning a gps. Manufacturers are conservative in their suggested accuracy of about 15 metres. Greater accuracy can usually be achieved between roughly 5–9 metres much of the time given a clear view of the sky. It is important to realise this EPE (Estimated Position Error) is only an estimate. Your current location can be given in a number of co-ordinate systems in the UK e.g. latitude and longitude or British Grid (see page 78). The diagram shows a location expressed in latitude and longitude. Your choice will depend upon where you are in the world, the maps you are using and which system you feel comfortable with. Many models now have either basemaps or uploadable maps which enable you to see your position on the screen.

2 Altitude (elevation)

Your gps receiver will give you your current altitude. Unfortunately this reading can be more erratic and cannot be relied upon but the reading is usually within about 15–25 metres of the true altitude when it settles down. Knowing your altitude to help pinpoint your position on a map can be important especially in bad weather when ascending or descending a mountain slope. You may find using an aeronoid altimeter gives a more reliable reading but it can be useful to compare it with a gps, though treat the gps reading with caution.

3 Direction of travel

Your receiver direction arrow (pointer) will point to your direction of travel but only when you are moving. You walk in the direction it points towards: your destination.

Your receiver direction arrow (pointer) will point to your direction of travel *but only when you are moving.* You walk in the direction it points towards: your destination.

The illustration shows the waypoint 'home' selected (with its symbol) and the pointer or arrow guides you to it. The compass ring gives compass references when you are on the move. In newer units the direction-of-travel arrow is more stable and can be relied upon when you are travelling in excess of 3–5 kilometres (2–3 miles) an hour. This can be a limitation in, say, rugged mountain terrain where progress can be slow. There are units with built-in electronic compasses (and altimeters) that will give you a direction even when you are stationary but they consume more battery power and are more expensive. Using a conventional compass saves the extra cost of these features.

4 A record of where you have walked

When you move with your gps switched on it will record an electronic 'breadcrumb' trail of the route you cover (remember to clear the tracklog memory before you set out). You can use this to retrace your steps, invaluable if you get lost. You save the tracklog and tell your receiver to guide you back (trackback) to your starting point. On your return home you can save your breadcrumb trail either to be used again or to upload to your computer where you can see where you have been on your digital map and analyse your walk. Some mapping programs will turn tracklogs into routes.

> When you move with your gps turned on it will record an electronic 'breadcrumb' trail of the route you cover. You can use this to retrace your steps, invaluable if you get lost.

Again your direction of travel arrow can only be relied on when you are moving. The points used to make up the breadcrumb trail of the tracklog (unlike waypoints) are anonymous, do not have names and cannot be easily individually accessed on your gps. You can work with them on some digital mapping programs.

5 Waypoints

You can enter into your gps grid references taken from a paper map of locations you want to visit. These are called waypoints. Waypoints can either be entered manually (or using a PC) into your gps or marked as an interesting location when out walking. Waypoints are the map co-ordinates of interesting locations worth recording. A waypoint has location and altitude recorded by your gps when you create it. A database of waypoints can be built up with names and symbols attached.

While waypoints can be manually entered into your receiver, named, given symbols and included in a route (the usual method if you are out walking), it is far easier to plan your routes on a PC and upload them to a gps receiver. This is covered in more detail later.

The illustration shows the waypoint 'mark' page. The location in the bottom window is expressed in latitude and longitude, the altitude (elevation) in feet. Inside the flag carried by the figure is the symbol (in this case, a little flag) and the default number given to the way-point by the gps receiver (in this case, 001). You can choose your own symbol from the options provided, plus name or number, grid system, and whether to use metric/statute units of measurement.

6 Other useful information

In addition to the information discussed already, most receivers give the total trip time, estimated time of arrival, distance walked, walking speed, average walking speed, the time of sunrise and sunset and very accurate time of day (using atomic clocks on the satellites). Apart from the time, and the time of sunrise and sunset, much of this latter data needs to be treated with caution. For various technical reasons they are not always accurate but are estimates based upon the best available data. In particular the receiver is measuring such things as Estimated Time of Arrival (ETA), or Time To Go (TTG) based on straight line paths, as the crow flies, to your destination, which is not how we walk but it is how the gps calculates when working with waypoints. Travelling in a boat or plane the ETA and TTG are more relevant.

More expensive units will have even more features and information than the entry level eTrex which can store 500 waypoints, 10 saved tracks and 20 routes. An example of a top of the range gps is the Garmin GPSmap 60CSx (page 77) which stores 1,000 waypoints, 20 tracks and 50 routes. It has a colour display, mapping facility, Atlantic basemap, an electronic compass giving you a heading while stationary, a barometric altimeter, expandable memory card, audible alarms and stopwatch, plus many other functions and information. For their mapping gps, Garmin sell their Topo Map of Great Britain, *based* on Ordnance Survey data, which aids navigation for walkers and

The pointer shows your direction of travel only when you are moving

motorists (page 50), but walkers should not expect the same level of
detail and information found on paper Ordnance Survey maps. You
may be satisfied with a basic gps, separate compass and altimeter
or you may prefer a more advanced unit like the 60CSx which
integrates these functions.

In challenging terrain even experienced walkers may feel incomplete
without a gps once they have used one to complement their
navigational skills. You need to be able to navigate conventionally to
fully exploit the potential of your gps. There is some resistance to
their use amongst navigational purists who seem to think using a gps
is cheating in some way. But the advantages of gps far outweigh
purist objections. Combined with guidebooks and maps, walking can
be more relaxing in unfamiliar terrain allowing a greater appreciation
of the scenery and the environment. Also you can cover ground
more quickly if you need to. Your gps can be of particular use in
some foreign countries where mapping is sometimes either poor
or non-existent. While navigating it is good practice to cross-check
all available information.

Understanding the limitations of gps receivers

- It is best to view your gps as *complementary* to your other navigational tools and not as a substitute. It is best used in conjunction with your map, compass and navigational skills. *You are strongly advised always to take the relevant paper maps with you on your walks.*

Tree cover can block reception

You need to be able to navigate conventionally to fully exploit the potential of your gps. You are strongly advised always to take the relevant paper maps with you on your walks.

You need a clear view of the sky to get a good locational fix and other data. In the UK it helps to have a clear sky view to the south. The satellites do not pass over the North Pole and so there is a 'hole' in the sky where there are no satellites. Mountains, cliffs, tree cover, buildings, your body: all these can block signal reception. As with mobile phones this can happen when you most need it. For all practical purposes your gps is not affected by weather or cloud cover.

- A gps receiver is an electronic device and can be damaged or go wrong, when you least expect it.

- It relies on battery power that runs down, hence the need to carry spares.

- Some receivers have maps but the display area is small and they are no substitute for paper maps which give a much better topographical overview.

- *There is a danger in taking readings at face value,* for example, in matters of distance and time which all units give. The gps calculates time based on straight-line progress to waypoints. In practice, of course, we do not get to our destinations by walking in straight lines. This is less of a problem for ships and aircraft where direct routes are more feasible. It is wise to treat a lot of the information provided as *estimates* although it is still very useful.

There is a danger in taking readings at face value, for example, in matters of distance and time which all units give. The gps calculations are based on straight-line progress to waypoints.

- The Americans developed the GPS system (NAVSTAR) for military purposes and still fund and control it. Theoretically they could turn it off. Some concern has been expressed about the ageing of the satellites and the upkeep of the system.

Starting off: initialising your receiver

A fter taking your new gps receiver out of the box and installing the batteries you will have to initialise it, that is, switch it on and let it receive signals from the satellites. Each satellite transmits its own positional information together with that of all the other satellites in the constellation. Your gps needs to obtain this information before it can calculate your position.

Take it outside with a clear view of the sky and keep it stationary. If it has a patch aerial (the eTrex does) it is best to keep it parallel to the ground and face upwards towards the sky. The gps stores the orbital information of the satellites. This orbital data is called the 'almanac'. Each satellite transmits its own orbital data approximately every 30 seconds and transmits the whole almanac of all the satellites every $12\frac{1}{2}$ minutes. If your receiver is left off for some time the almanac information becomes dated or 'cold' and it can take a little time to update. This is referred to as a 'cold start'. A 'warm start' is when the almanac has been updated within the last 4–6 hours. If the gps already has up-to-date information when switched on, it will lock on to the satellites' signals more quickly and so give you a more rapid reading of your location. Cold and warm start acquisition times are usually included in the gps manual or promotional literature.

Initialise your receiver out of doors

All that remains is 'setting it up' i.e. customising it so that it meets your needs and relates to the location and maps you will be using. You can use your gps receiver anywhere in the world so you have to make certain choices to adapt it to where you are. This is where you will need to refer to your manual. A typical set-up page will approximate to the following format which is based on the Garmin eTrex and recommendations apply to the UK using Ordnance Survey maps. You need to set up all gps receivers in a similar way.

> *You can use your gps receiver anywhere in the world so you have to make certain choices to adapt it to where you are.*

Set-up screen (accessed from the menu page on the eTrex)

Quick set-up recommendations illustrate the sort of decisions you will have to make in order for your gps to function in your current location.

Recommended settings for your receiver's essential functions for use in the UK

If you feel inclined to delve deeper into the meaning of the various settings please refer to the chapter which follows after this quick set-up guide (see bibliography to follow up the topics introduced).

Quick set-up page recommendations

Time: 12/24 hour clock to preference
Time zone: London
Daylight saving: automatic
Position format: British Grid
Map datum: OSGB (Magellan: GRB36)
Units of measurement: statute or metric to preference
North reference: grid north (to make it compatible with map readings) or magnetic north (to correspond with your compass). In practice it is probably best to use magnetic north.
Interface page (to communicate with your PC): Garmin. (Magellan: NMEA)
System page: normal

A closer look at setting up your receiver

1 Time format

Receivers obtain very accurate time data transmitted from atomic clocks (accurate to within one second every million years) on the satellites. A gps receiver when receiving signals from the satellites is probably your most accurate timepiece.

You will need to choose:
- between a 12- and 24-hour time display
- the time zone in which you will be walking: London
- daylight saving time: automatic.

2 Display page

The display page allows you to choose the length of time the back light stays on. This enables you to see the screen at night or in poor lighting conditions. Also it is here that you may adjust the screen contrast making the display lighter or darker.

3 Position format (grid system)

The position format is the co-ordinate or grid system employed by the map you are using and which hopefully is identified somewhere on the map. A co-ordinate system is a way of describing locations on a map. There are many co-ordinate systems in use around the world and a given map may have a number of co-ordinate systems. Ordnance Survey maps have a grid made up of numbered faint blue lines drawn running north/south and east/west which allow you to pinpoint a location. This is the OSBG or Ordnance Survey British Grid. On these maps you will also find a grid of latitude and longitude, the oldest map co-ordinate system, indicated along the outer edges of the map. So you could use latitude and longitude with Ordnance Survey maps but we recommend OSBG which is easier to deal with. The basic eTrex has 18 different grids for use in different parts of the world. The default position format (co-ordinate system) is latitude and longitude. There is also an option that allows advanced users to use custom-designed grids. Make sure when you buy a receiver that it has latitude and longitude, UTM/UPS, and a grid relevant to any country you intend visiting. For the UK you need British Grid.

4 Map datum (reference position)

The subject of map datums is complex, involving sophisticated mathematics. Countries base their maps on different mathematical models and projections representing the shape of the earth's surface. Each model is a map datum. For each datum, locations are referenced to a given 'origin' point so that every point on the map is a known distance and height from that 'origin'. You need to see if the map you are using has datum information printed on it. This information is essential whenever you are going to relate gps data to paper maps. You must then use the correct grid and datum relevant to your map or you could produce serious errors in your positioning. (See helpful explanation of datums at: www.gpsu.co.uk/datums.html.)

In the UK the datum is Ordnance Survey Great Britain (OSGB) and this is the datum you select when using Ordnance Survey maps. We are fortunate in the UK in having only one datum (since 1936). You will find this statement in the legend at the bottom of Ordnance Survey maps: 'Base map constructed on Transverse Mercator projection, Airy Spheroid, OSGB (1936) Datum. Vertical datum mean sea level (Newlyn).'

The default datum on your gps is WGS84 (World Geodetic System 1984). Make sure the gps you buy supports the datum of the areas you want to walk in. Receivers usually have a good list of commonly used datums but check all the same.

On the basic eTrex you first choose your grid system (position format) and it will automatically choose an appropriate datum.

5 Units of measurement

The options here are:
- nautical (knots)
- statute (feet and miles)
- metric (metres and kilometres). Ordnance Survey use metric measurements.

We recommend metric but it is a question of personal preference and habit.

6 The three north references

There are three 'norths' you need to have a working knowledge of. This is because map-makers have to represent the spheroid Earth on a flat plane, i.e. piece of paper. They are illustrated in the diagram and you will find them marked in the map legend on Ordnance Survey maps just like this.

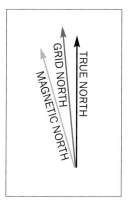

- **True north:** the direction from any place on Earth to the North Pole or the top of the Earth's vertical axis upon which it rotates. You can also think of it as the north direction of a line of longitude. Map-makers try to align the grid lines on their maps with true north. If you select this setting your gps shows bearings with reference to the North Pole. When it gives a bearing of '0' degrees you are on your way to the North Pole whereas a bearing of 180 degrees sets you off in the opposite direction, to the South Pole.

- **Grid north:** refers to the direction of the vertical grid lines running from the bottom to the top of the map. Distortions inherent in the process of representing the Earth on a flat surface (piece of paper) result in grid lines not pointing exactly to the North Pole. This gives us the concept of grid north. If you set your gps to grid north it will correspond to grid north on the map.

In the UK grid north is equal to true north at longitude 2 degrees west. This is the central meridian: it passes through Poole in Dorset and

Berwick-on-Tweed. Grid lines are parallel to each other but lines of longitude converge and meet at the North Pole hence any north/south grid line not on the central meridian is not pointing to true north.

For practical purposes two of the three norths can be used for setting up your receiver: grid north and magnetic north.

- **Magnetic north:** the direction your compass needle points towards. A compass needle always points to magnetic north which is presently found south east of the north pole in northern Canada. 'Magnetic North moves slowly with a variable rate and currently is west of Grid North in Great Britain' (Ordnance Survey).

- **Magnetic variation:** 'The horizontal angular difference between True North and Magnetic North is called **Magnetic Variation** or **Declination**. The horizontal angular difference between Grid North and Magnetic North is called **Grid Magnetic Angle**. It is this angle which needs to be applied when converting between magnetic and grid bearing' (Ordnance Survey). In Britain 'magnetic variation' is sometimes taken to mean the difference between magnetic north and either grid north or true north. Look at your Ordnance Survey map margin for details of magnetic variation relevant at the time of the map's publication. Up-to-date information for the area in which you wish to walk can be obtained from the Ordnance Survey or British Geological Survey (Tel: 0131 6671000 or via their website www.geomag.bgs.ac.uk/uksurvey.html). Magnetic variation changes as you travel round the world: in Britain it is comparatively quite small. You can program your gps to display either grid or magnetic north and it will automatically make the adjustment.

You will find information on the three 'norths' in the marginal information on Ordnance Survey maps. For example, the Ordnance Survey Gloucester, Cheltenham and Stroud, Explorer Map 179 1:25 000 scale states: 'At the centre of this sheet true north is 0° 08' east of grid north. Magnetic north is estimated at 2° 47' west of grid north for Jul. 2007. Annual change is approximately 09' east. Magnetic data supplied by the British Geological Survey'.

> *If you want your gps to relate to your map set it to grid north; set it to magnetic north if you want to use it in conjunction with your compass.*

So if you want your gps to relate directly to your map set it to grid north; set it to magnetic north if you want to use it in conjunction with your compass.

7 Interface page (PC connection)

This is where you can set your receiver to communicate with other devices, the most important of which is your computer. You can transfer waypoints, routes and tracks between computer and gps receiver. Choose Garmin for Garmin receivers and NMEA for Magellan. See your manual for further details.

8 System page

Here you find the details of the software version installed on your receiver. You can find relevant updates on the manufacturer's website.

- **Normal mode:** in this setting the gps is switched on all the time when in use and is more sensitive to sudden turns or changes in speed and acceleration while you are moving. However, this uses more power from your batteries than in battery save.

- **Battery save:** this switches the receiver on and off at intervals to save battery power but it will be less sensitive to your every movement. Not the best setting if you are using WAAS/EGNOS.

- **Demo mode:** allows you to switch between the various screens and functions with the gps turned off, i.e. it does not try to receive data from the satellites. A useful setting while you are learning. Retailers use it to demonstrate their wares. Clearly you cannot navigate in this setting.

The Garmin eTrex: an illustrated look at the five main screens or pages

The five main screens on the basic Garmin eTrex

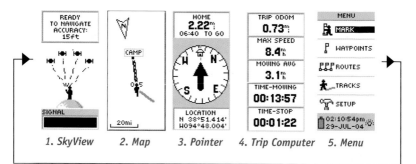

1. SkyView   2. Map   3. Pointer   4. Trip Computer   5. Menu

The five screens

This example uses the entry level Garmin to illustrate some of the typical screens or 'pages' found on most gps receivers. The information may be laid out a little differently on other models and makes but it will be essentially the same. More expensive gps receivers will have more functions but this does mean it takes more time and effort to plumb their depths and to come to terms with how they work. As stated earlier the eTrex has the virtue of being simple, straightforward and aimed at walkers. If you grasp the essence of what is described you will, with a little practice in the field, be able to operate any gps. You will find using them a lot of fun.

Let us look at the five main screens or pages that can be called upon: the satellite, map, pointer or navigation, trip computer and menu pages. Let us have a brief look at each in turn.

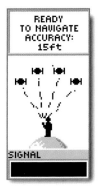

1 The SkyView screen

When you first power up your gps the SkyView page is the first one to come up on the eTrex. It will show your current relationship with the orbiting satellites and the strength of the signal being received. You can choose between the two screens illustrated, the SkyView Page (left) and the Advanced SkyView Page (below).

The status window at the top indicates when your receiver has made contact with sufficient satellites and is 'ready to navigate'. It also gives an indication of the estimated accuracy (estimated position error or EPE) of your present position in the measurement system you have chosen.

Manufacturers state this is within 10–15 metres but you can often do better than this. But remember it is only an estimate. The bottom window displays a bar showing the strength of the signal being received at a given time.

Underneath the status window on the Advanced SkyView Page is a number of concentric circles with figures scattered around them. These are the numbered satellites in contact range of your present location. The outer circle represents the horizon, the inner circle represents the sky above you at an angle of 45 degrees from vertical whilst the centre is the sky directly overhead. As contact is made with the satellites the numbers are given a black background.

The bottom of the page shows a bar graph with the satellite numbers on the horizontal axis. At first the bars are empty, but as contact is made they become filled in. The height of each bar indicates the strength of the signal being received. In practice you will see them fluctuating up and down, hovering around a particular height. Your gps needs contact with at least four satellites to get a 3-D fix and the aim of the satellite system is to make available at least four satellites in the sky wherever you are. For a good fix the satellites should be well spaced and no three in a straight line.

The standard satellites are numbered between one and 32. Any number above this represents satellites used for WAAS correction. When your gps is receiving a WAAS/EGNOS signal either a small 'D ' (differential signal) or a 'W' (WAAS signal) appears on the bars of the relevant satellites.

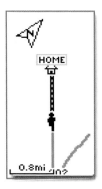

2 The Map screen

The Map Page is a very useful one and one you may use a lot. 'Map Page' is a misnomer because it is rather a graphic representation or a schematic map. It helps you to orientate yourself and to navigate and can be of particular importance at junctions. The map shows you where you have been and where you plan to travel. It shows a figure walking, you at your current location, leaving a breadcrumb trail or tracklog as you progress along your path which projects forward ahead of the figure to your destination. The walking man symbol is animated when you move (the moving figure is a Garmin feature). Waypoints with their names and symbols appear on the map as you progress from waypoint to waypoint when you are following a route. When you are using the trackback function, the tracklog is displayed on the screen showing your progress along it and any waypoints you have created. If you walk off the tracklog you can witness this happening as a breadcrumb trail is created showing your movement in relation to the saved tracklog.

You may customise the map display choosing from a number of options. For example, you can either have the top of your screen showing the direction in which you are heading or have it pointing north like a paper map. The map scale can be altered as well. If a question mark appears it means satellite reception has been lost and you need a clearer view of the sky to regain it.

3 The Pointer or Navigation screen

This page aids your active navigation on your walk. Garmin have called this the 'Pointer Page' rather than the 'Compass Page' to emphasise, possibly, that it is not actually a compass although it does give you compass directions when you are on the move.

When you have selected a waypoint, route or tracklog to follow, the arrow (pointer) indicates the direction of travel and an outer 'compass' ring gives you compass references but remember both are active only when you are moving. If you are following a route your gps shows the next waypoint and symbol (if you have given the waypoint a symbol) to which you are being 'pointed' or directed.

> *When you have selected a waypoint, route or tracklog to follow, the arrow (pointer) indicates the direction of travel and an outer 'compass' ring gives you compass references but remember both are active only when you are moving.*

The Pointer Page
The top window shows the next waypoint with the straight line distance to it and estimated straight line time of arrival (ETA).

At the bottom of this page you have access to a menu of data. You may choose one of the following to be displayed at any one time:

- **speed** (how fast you are walking)
- **average speed** (average speed walked)
- **maximum speed** (maximum speed walked)
- **heading** (the compass direction you are walking in)
- **bearing** (compass reading to your next waypoint)
- **elevation** (your current altitude)
- **location** (gives you your OSBG 10-figure grid reference, if using this grid system)
- **sunrise** (at your present position)

- **sunset** (at your present position)
- **trip time** (the time you have been walking)
- **trip odometer** (the total time walked since you last reset it).

Note: the pointer or arrow (destination symbol and bearing) will only be present on the screen when you are following a GOTO (moving to a selected waypoint), a route or tracklog. The 'moving direction line' (the short vertical line to the top of the compass ring in the diagram) will indicate your direction on the compass ring as long as you are moving.

4 The Trip Computer screen

The trip computer provides you with information about your walking. There are five windows that can be customised from a list of data fields but do not be too impressed with this welter of information because as a walker you are unlikely to need most of it. Some of this information is available on the pointer page but it is convenient to have a collection of informative data available at a glance. In practice you may find you use altitude, bearing, clock time, distance walked and above all, location. The time of sunset will be accurate and important in ensuring you complete your outing in daylight. As we have already explained, a lot of this information needs to be handled with care and not taken too literally.

5 The Menu screen

This page allows you to enter the heart of your gps and gives access to its advanced features. The data is organised under the five categories illustrated. From this screen or page you can create or 'mark' waypoints, enter the waypoint database of waypoints already stored, construct your routes, save and review your tracklogs and customise your screen displays and various other information, from the choices available in 'set-up', necessary for the functioning of your receiver.

On the basic eTrex matters are not too complex. On other Garmin models and those of different manufacturers you will find the data set out differently but the underlying principles and information are the same. The detail and range of possibilities are likely to be greater on more advanced and expensive receivers. There will be more to take on board but once you have got a feel for what is going on things will become clearer much more quickly. You will not find any gps receiver intrinsically difficult to master but it will take a little time and practice.

At the bottom of the page is a battery gauge that shows you the state of your batteries. When you put in freshly charged rechargeable batteries they will tend to register less than full. This is a characteristic of rechargeable batteries. It is probably a good idea to remove the batteries if you are not going to use your unit for a long time. Removing the batteries will not cause a loss of stored data.

Always check the state of your batteries before setting out on a hike.

There is also a screen backlight indicator that shows whether it is on or off. The time and date are also found here.

Explore your data, expand your horizons

The gps
in action

There are three main ways you can use your gps to guide you on a walk:

1 The GOTO

2 The ROUTE

3 The TRACKBACK

1 The GOTO function

The GOTO function allows you to tell your gps to direct you to a single waypoint chosen from the database of waypoints stored on your gps. It is important to stress that your receiver will give you a straight line direction to your waypoint: fine at sea but needs using with care on land. There may be a cliff or river or some other hazard between you and your destination. The pointer (arrow) will always point to the selected waypoint, so even if you cannot walk in a straight line you can work your way towards it in the best way you can. This works really well. Your gps will update the compass bearing to the waypoint from wherever you are.

You can rarely walk just in straight lines

Some receivers have a separate 'man overboard' key (MOB) which when pressed permits an instant recording of a location (i.e. creation of a waypoint) and return to it. The maritime origins and purpose are obvious. This is often useful if you park your car in a strange location at the beginning of a walk. As soon as you get out of your car, mark the position with the MOB function or just create a waypoint.

2 The ROUTE function

A route is a plan of where you want to go whereas a track (see next) is a record of where you have been. Your route will be made up of a sequential series of waypoints. The receiver guides you waypoint to waypoint. You can use the pointer page (screen) to follow the arrow. The map page will display the route and its waypoints, indicating your progress along it. Additionally a lot of other very useful information will be provided such as compass bearing to next waypoint, its straight line

> *A route is a plan of where you want to go whereas a track is a record of where you have been. Your route will be made up of a sequential series of waypoints. The receiver guides you waypoint to waypoint.*

distance and estimated time of arrival. Your receiver allows you to name, store, reverse and modify routes. You will need to refer to your manual to see how these operations are carried out but they are usually very simple to perform. It is worth noting that if you delete a waypoint from your gps database it will be deleted from all routes of which it might form a part.

Creating a route

There are a number of ways to create a route:

- You could read grid references off a paper map and enter them into your receiver manually. This is rather like writing a text message on a mobile phone. Without the use of a PC, or if you are out in the field, this is the way you have to enter waypoints.

- You could build a route in your gps made up of waypoints already in your receiver's database using its route creation function.

- You can use your PC and one of the 'stand-alone' programs like GPSUtility, OziExplorer or EasyGPS (see page 51). Look up your references on a paper map, type them into the software and with a click of the mouse transfer them to your receiver: this is quicker and more accurate than entering them manually. If you have a scanner and the expertise, scan a section of map into your PC and then trace out your route creating waypoints which can then be transferred to your receiver. Be aware of copyright issues. You will need to connect your gps to your computer.

- You can buy one of the proprietary PC programs produced by firms like Anquet Technology Ltd or Memory-Map where you will plan your walks on full colour Ordnance Survey maps on your PC screen. The drawback with this option is that they are quite expensive to buy although you may find they are cost effective in the long run when compared with buying paper maps.

Whatever method you have used to put together your route, your gps will guide you waypoint to waypoint providing information on the next destination waypoint. It is as well to be aware that in some circumstances your gps can skip a waypoint or lock onto a 'wrong' waypoint. For example, at the beginning of a circular walk double check that your gps is directing you to your first rather than your last waypoint. It is best not to create waypoints too close together. Always check which waypoint you are being directed to. In situations where it

> *In situations where it is important to reach a given waypoint you might consider switching your receiver to its GOTO function.*

is important to reach a given waypoint you might consider switching your receiver to its GOTO function. You can always return to following your original route after arriving at the waypoint.

If you are following a route and decide to switch off your gps, perhaps to save battery power, it will pick up your route when you switch it on again and resume guiding you from your present location.

The number of waypoints you include in a route will of course depend on the complexity of the route and your own needs. Probably you will need fewer than you might think. Experience will show you how many you find appropriate.

You may find it useful to either use a laminated map, or paper maps printed off from your digital mapping programs, and a marker pen to periodically mark in your positions as given by your gps. This helps you to always know roughly where you are as you walk and will help keep you on route with the knowledge of where you are on the map.

Something worth remembering is that a gps unit is not completely accurate, with most claiming accuracy in the region of 10–15 metres. If you can imagine this error as a circle around your true position, then you should be able to visualise that navigating using your gps to a waypoint within that circle could well be compromised by the error. In extreme cases, the pointer could be pointing the wrong way. For instance, imagine you are physically one metre south of the waypoint you are navigating to. Your gps should have a pointer pointing north telling you that you need to walk one metre north. However, if the gps thinks you are two metres north of the waypoint (i.e. a three metre error from your real position – well within the error margin stated), then the gps will tell you that you need to walk south two metres to reach your waypoint. Most gps give you an estimated positional error that is related to the probable accuracy of your position that you can take into account in your navigation at any given time. In difficult conditions you should be aware of the possible errors in your gps position.

Waypoint management

Your receiver allows you to build up a database of waypoints, typically about 500. Waypoints are the co-ordinates of locations saved in your gps's memory. Waypoints or landmarks are the basis of gps operation. When you create a waypoint the default gps name will be 001, 002 and so on. You can identify these further by giving them a name and/or symbol.

After a while it can become difficult to manage the increasing number of waypoints you will accumulate in your gps database or to find a particular one unless you have given it a name and/or symbol. Out in the field it is sometimes simpler just to jot down the name and number of each waypoint in a small notebook instead. Either way, you will need to remind yourself where you created a waypoint and the feature it represents.

Some gps have databases of waypoints pre-installed when you buy them. These 'points of interest' (POIs) contain airports, restaurants, hotels or road junctions together with lists of major towns. Usually it is not possible to edit these lists.

Nearest waypoints

Many receivers provide you with a list of the nearest waypoints. The eTrex gives you the nine nearest to your current position with details of their location and altitude. They will come up on your map page. These could be of use if you become disoriented.

Entering waypoints into your gps manually

You may assemble a list of waypoints for inclusion in a route by reading the references from a map, taking them from a walking magazine or guidebook, or via your PC (lists of waypoints are available on the Internet). Using gps software is discussed later. We will consider entering waypoints manually into your gps that can then be constructed into a route on your gps.

In the Garmin eTrex (other models and makes will be broadly similar) there are two ways to input waypoints manually:

- *If you want to enter a waypoint while on a walk:* with your receiver switched on, hold down the 'enter key' on any screen (page). You can also use the dedicated 'Mark' screen and a way-point of your present location with co-ordinates and altitude (elevation) will be created while you are walking. The gps gives it a default number (001, 002 and so on) or you can give it your own name and symbol. Some receivers have a special dedicated key to do this.

- *If you want to enter a waypoint(s) from a list:* with your gps switched either on or in 'demonstration mode', where the gps function is off, go to the Menu Page and 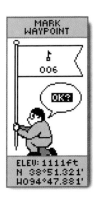 choose 'Mark'. When you first call up the 'Mark Page' a reference will already be at the bottom of the page. You need to overwrite this creating your new waypoint co-ordinates. Highlight the reference and press enter. Now overwrite each digit selecting each letter/number separately and replace it with the details of the new grid reference and 'Okay' it (see page 81). Take extra care when entering the numbers because errors could result in wrong locations.

Following a route

Where do you place waypoints?

As you already know, waypoints are important in gps navigation and route planning – but where do you put your waypoints? It is difficult to lay down any hard and fast rules about this. The placing and number of waypoints you use in planning a walk will depend on a number of factors, e.g. the nature of the walk, expected weather conditions and your personal needs. Some people like a lot of way-points, others manage on far fewer. Some walkers use a number of waypoints, distributed on prominent features like hills or mountain tops, for reference purposes. Continental maps of mountain areas often mark significant features with co-ordinates and you can use these as waypoints.

To start you off, here are a few questions to think about.

1. You need to turn right. Where would you put your waypoints at this crucial junction?

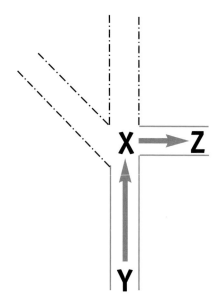

Many people would put it at X. However, it might be better to put a waypoint at Y and/or Z as well or instead. Which of these waypoints would you use and why?

2. On the right is another example. Your path is ahead. *A lot of paths crisscross at this junction.* Again many people might put a waypoint at X. Where would you put your waypoint(s)? It might be better to put one before the junction at Y to alert you that it is coming up and

perhaps one afterwards at Z to navigate you through the confusion of paths. This might be important if you were expecting mist or low cloud which would obscure the track ahead. If you have got a straight bit of path after the junction, the farther the waypoint Z is from X, the more accurate your pointer will be.

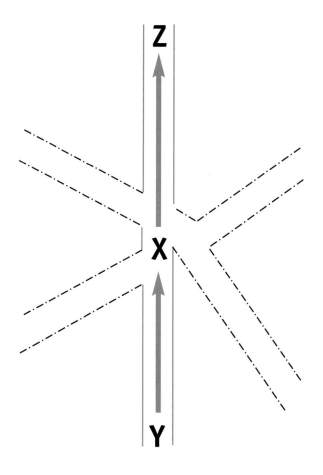

3 The TRACKBACK function

One of the really useful things your gps can do for you is to record your progress as you move along your path with a 'breadcrumb' trail. It is rather like leaving a paper trail as you walk along. Each trackpoint's location, time and altitude are recorded but are not accessible on your receiver. As you move along your path, your gps will lay down trackpoints (breadcrumbs) at given intervals of time or distance according to the options you have selected. If set to 'automatic', then the gps will choose when to record a trackpoint. When the track memory is full, you have two options: either to record over previously recorded tracks or to stop recording at this point.

If you refer to your map page you can see the breadcrumb trail being built up as you walk. If for any reason you lose contact with the satellites (perhaps by switching your receiver on and off to conserve battery power or passing under dense tree cover), the recording of your breadcrumb trail will cease. There will be a break in your tracklog until you get reception again. Your receiver will record a discontinuous log but when saved it will be joined up as a continuous tracklog.

Should you need to retrace your steps you can save your active tracklog, select it and activate *the trackback function*. Your gps will then lead you back the way you came. In fact, you are able to re-walk

Tracklog can be reassuring in featureless terrain

the tracklog in either direction after you have saved it. This option can be very reassuring in difficult terrain. It is best not to have your gps on battery save mode while you are recording a tracklog because it will be less sensitive to the twists and turns of your path. Your gps will let you save, store and name tracklogs for future use.

Having saved the tracklog on your gps and started a trackback you can see your tracklog displayed on the map page. You can follow your progress along your saved tracklog on the map screen as you retrace your steps. You can clearly see any deviations from your tracklog when you are re-walking it because you will be laying down yet another breadcrumb trail which you can see departing from it. Information concerning individual trackpoints is inaccessible on your gps although some gps software allows you to access trackpoint information on your PC.

For added reassurance on a difficult trail you can create waypoints at intervals even though you are creating a tracklog. Waypoints will be positioned along the tracklog and displayed on the map page. In contrast to trackpoints you can select a waypoint on your gps with its accompanying information on its location and altitude. However there are many more trackpoints recorded in the tracklog than you would have waypoints in a route. Consequently when following a trackback your gps should give better directions than walking a route which simply shows straight lines, waypoint to waypoint.

On your return home, if you have a PC with the appropriate software, you can download your tracklog and compare your actual walked path with the route you had planned. If you intend downloading it to your computer it is best not to save it on your gps beforehand as some receivers will reduce the number of track points recorded in order to save memory (and strip out trackpoint recorded times). Tracklogs can be turned into routes on some PC programs.

A point worth noting: if you turn your receiver on at home in order to check it and then later in the day start your walk at another place, you will, if and when you download it to a digital map on your PC, get a track line on your PC from home to the start of your walk. This is messy so it is best to check your receiver indoors. That way it cannot locate the satellites. Alternatively check and clear the memory when you arrive at the start of your walk. You will need to check that the track feature is enabled before setting out.

Before embarking on a demanding walk in unfamiliar or featureless country, clear the tracklog memory (do not forget to do this) and allow your receiver to record your journey, creating waypoints at critical points along the way. You can then be confident that, should you need to retrace your steps for any reason, your eTrex will enable you to do so. You must first save the tracklog and then instruct your receiver to trackback to the beginning of your walk. It will with surprising accuracy guide you back over the twists and turns of your previously walked path. You follow the pointer (arrow) on the pointer page that also gives you information about the distance to cover, estimated time of arrival, together with the information you select, such as location or heading. You can also turn to the map page where you can see your breadcrumb trail with the waypoints you have created scattered along its course and follow your progress as you walk. The map screen is very useful and you may use it a great deal. It will also show you on a trackback, by means of the breadcrumb trail, where you are departing from your tracklog.

> *A gps can be very useful even if you have no maps of where you are. You can still use your gps and its tracklog to record your journey.*

A gps can be very useful even if you have no maps of where you are. You can still use your gps and its tracklog to record your journey. Make sure you have cleared your track memory and turned on the track function before setting out. Then if you need to, you can always follow your track back to your starting point. On the return journey you will be able to see your current position relative to your outbound track. This can be very reassuring when you are walking in challenging, unfamiliar terrain, perhaps abroad.

Improving the accuracy of your gps: WAAS/EGNOS

WAAS is short for Wide Area Augmentation System. Again it is a system of satellites and ground stations developed by the Americans in order to 'augment' the accuracy of GPS signals. Essentially WAAS, where available, provides greater precision and accuracy for the use of aircraft and shipping. It is fully operational but only available in North America. Descriptions of the system in your gps manual will reflect its American origin.

However, a complementary system is being developed in Europe, EGNOS (European Geostationary Navigation Overlay Service), which will provide a similar service for most of Europe. *'EGNOS is Europe's first step in satellite navigation, paving the way for Galileo, the future civil Global Positioning System' (British National Space Centre, 2005).* Galileo was planned to be operational by 2008 but recent authorative estimates have put it back to 2010–11. When fully operational it is claimed accuracy will be improved to within one metre.

What does all this mean for the leisure user? Well firstly, access to the system is free and when EGNOS becomes fully available the position accuracy of receivers for Europeans will improve from the present 7–15 metres to between 3–5 metres, 95 per cent of the time. EGNOS is transmitting test signals at the time of writing and estimates are that the system will become fully operational sometime in 2006.

EGNOS is Europe's first step in satellite navigation, paving the way for Galileo, the future civil GPS. So in terms of your manual, instructions relating to WAAS can be read as applying to EGNOS reception when it becomes fully available.

You will need a clear view of the sky to make best use of the signal. In the UK you will need a view of the southern sky. So in terms of your manual, instructions relating to WAAS can be read as applying to EGNOS reception when it becomes fully available. On the eTrex you can turn WAAS/EGNOS on and off. Until EGNOS is fully operational it is probably better to keep it turned off.

Your satellite reception page on the eTrex receiver will indicate when your signal is being improved by WAAS/EGNOS by displaying a 'D' in the satellite strength bar indicators.

There are other ways of improving the accuracy of your gps but they are probably only of academic interest to most walkers. Your signal reception can be enhanced by connecting an external aerial. DGPS (Differential GPS) gives greater precision to people like surveyors who need a high degree of accuracy in their work. Should you need to use the DGPS correctional signals you would have to attach a separate beacon receiver to your gps (if DGPS compatible).

Batteries and your gps

When you are out with your gps you will have to rely on battery power, usually from two AA or three AAA batteries. Some receivers have rechargeable lithium batteries but spares tend to be expensive and not as readily available as AA batteries. Manufacturers specify an expected battery life ranging between 12–22 hours for the sort of units under consideration. The actual life in the field will depend on the features used on your gps receiver and the type of batteries. Use of backlights and electronic compasses (if a feature) make big demands on batteries. Some receivers come with a 'battery save' mode that extends battery life but when switched on can make the unit a little less sensitive. All receivers have a gauge that tells you the current state of your batteries although they do vary in their accuracy and you need to discover the foibles of your receiver before trusting it.

eTrex battery compartment

Rechargeable batteries will work out cheaper in the long run and are friendlier to the environment. They do not have the charge of good quality non-rechargeable alkaline batteries like Duracell and run down over time when stored, so always check them before going out. Nickel Metal Hydride (NiMH) are the best: they do not have the 'memory' problem of Nickel Cadmium (NiCad) ones, which need to be completely exhausted before recharging or their charge capacity is adversely affected. Manufacturers claim that NiMH batteries are typically rechargeable up to about 1,000 times. You could use good quality NiMH batteries and carry some alkaline (Duracell) ones just in case.

> *Changing the batteries in the middle of navigation does not result in the loss of information.*

In some receivers you can specify which type of battery is being used. The wrong setting only affects the accuracy of your battery gauge because different batteries have different discharge rates. Most receivers will warn you when your batteries are running low. Changing the batteries in the middle of navigating does not result in the loss of information, so do not worry about that.

Gps and digital maps

Gps mapping programs

You could use your gps without maps. You could just use the tracklog function that might be useful in some circumstances but clearly you would get more out of your gps in conjunction with maps, as we have already seen. Paper maps can be used to work out grid references which can then be entered manually into your gps as waypoints, built up into routes and so on. Recent developments in gps software and digital maps for the PC have opened up new horizons, greatly increasing the ease and power of gps navigation.

A number of software programs are now available, some as free downloads from the Internet, which make it much easier to enter grid references into your gps and create waypoints, routes and tracks. Some of these programs also allow you to scan in and digitise sections of maps. You will need to connect your gps to your computer to take advantage of this software. Some newer receivers may be able to connect via 'Bluetooth' (a wireless equivalent to a cable).

Broadly speaking there are three kinds of gps software you can use on your PC with your gps receiver:

1 Software programs produced by gps manufacturers

The major gps manufacturers produce their own mapping software and maps. Magellan products are called *MapSend,* Lowrance call theirs *MapCreate* and Garmin mapping software is called *MapSource.* Each manufacturer produces a variety of maps ranging from marine charts to topographical and street maps. Garmin and Magellan sell maps of Britain *based* on Ordnance Survey mapping for use on their gps. The programs allow you to view the maps on your PC where you can create waypoints and routes to transfer to your gps.

If you have a gps with mapping capability you can upload sections of maps to it. These more expensive units will often have basemaps already loaded in their memory when you buy them of, for example, Europe. Do not expect too much from the basemaps on your gps as they do not compare with their paper cousins either in accuracy or readability. If you want a gps with mapping make sure you get as big a memory as you can afford with at least 32MB.

Your gps screen is very small and unless you have a colour gps it can be quite difficult to use. Digital maps really come into their own on your PC where you have a large viewing area and full colour.

The important thing to stress about these mapping programs and maps is that they are compatible *only* with the gps of the company which produced them, i.e. on Garmin gps receivers you can only use Garmin *MapSource.* In other words you cannot upload maps of any kind to your gps other than ones produced by their manufacturer. Perhaps it is also important to emphasise that you cannot use maps on all models of gps, only on those that are specifically designed for this purpose.

2 Software produced by digital mapping companies

There are a number of digital mapping programs for sale on CD-ROM or DVD that combined with your gps add an exciting dimension to walking in the UK.

The leading brands at present are TrackLogs, Fugawi, Memory-Map and Anquet. All use Ordnance Survey maps under licence: the differences come in the way they operate. Essentially they all do the same job and your choice will depend on personal preference and whether their mapping meets your needs. You can sample their products by exploring their websites or requesting a demonstration CD-ROM. At present cost is a major drawback of this software but with a growing market prices should come down. Two competing products, those produced by Anquet and Memory-Map, are both very good. We will use Anquet mapping as an example to discuss in more detail later (see page 53).

3 Stand-alone software programs available on the Internet

There are programs that in many ways resemble the software described previously but they do not have maps included (see page 55). It is probably true to say they are not as easy to use either. If you want to exploit their mapping potential you have to scan areas of map into the software on your PC. In the jargon they are known as 'stand-alone' programs. Amongst the more well-known programs are *OziExplorer* and *GPS Utility* but there are others and each has its adherents. In summary these gps programs allow you to:

- At their simplest, type a list of waypoint co-ordinates into your PC and then upload them to your gps: much easier and quicker than doing it manually. You can then construct routes on your gps or use the GOTO function.

- Scan in a section of map and with a click of your mouse get the grid reference at the cursor's location and create a waypoint. Routes and tracks can be planned and instantly uploaded to your gps. After walks you can download your data into your PC and work with it in a number of ways: there are many other functions available in these powerful programs.

- Use 'tracklog navigation'. You have seen how you can record a walk on your gps and make a tracklog to be subsequently re-walked. With this gps software you are able to draw a track on a scanned-in section of map and upload it into your gps as a tracklog ready to be walked. *It is not necessary to have walked the route beforehand.* Additionally, if you are limited in the number of routes you can store on your gps, you are now able to store walks as tracklogs in the tracklog memory.

The tracklogs so constructed allow 'tracklog navigation.' This enables closer guidance from your gps owing to the fact that there are typically more trackpoints in a tracklog than waypoints in a route. However, in contrast to waypoints you cannot access information about trackpoints on your gps.

There are other free programs that can be downloaded from the Internet which are not mapping software but which allow you to transfer data between your gps and computer and manage your waypoints, tracks and routes. Good examples of these are *G7ToWin* and *EasyGps*. Also of interest are a number of websites where you can download maps. Many are American but you can get useful maps from UK websites such as Multimap and Street Map.

'Tracklog navigation': with this gps software you are able to draw a track on a scanned-in section of map and upload it into your gps as a tracklog ready to be walked. It is not necessary to have walked the route beforehand.

You will have gathered by now that the Internet is a rich source of information and programs that can add greatly to what you can do with your gps receiver (see page 91 for details).

Google Earth

A special mention should be made of Google Earth, an amazing resource freely available on the Internet as long as you have Broadband. *'Google Earth combines satellite imagery, maps and the power of Google Search to put the world's geographic information at your finger-tips' (Google).* It allows you to 'virtually' travel anywhere in the world and zoom in on a particular location. You can see fields, mountains, cities and, in some well photographed areas, even cars, houses and road markings. The 'terrain' function gives 3-D impressions that can be tilted and moved, allowing you to fly down the Grand Canyon or explore Mount Everest. You can use this facility to visualise, explore or check a proposed route before you actually walk it.

So detailed is the imagery that some authorities have become alarmed and have expressed fears about security. It will find destinations like roads, specific addresses and restaurants and you can add personalised 'place markers' and create tours. You can also print off maps. An up-grade is available which allows the import of data (waypoints, routes and tracks) from Garmin and Magellan gps receivers although you cannot export data from Google Earth to your gps. Some of the CDs of walks that are beginning to accompany walking guides allow the transfer of their walks to Google Earth where you can fly over them in virtual reality. You can use GPS Utility to convert files to Google Earth (KML) files. You will find a visit to the Google Earth website rewarding: www.earth.google.com

An example of software produced by a digital mapping company

Anquet Technology Ltd is a high-tech company based in London, producing cutting edge digital mapping software. Currently their product range includes Ordnance Survey 1:50 000 and 1:25 000 mapping of the UK which can be combined with a separate series of aerial photo maps covering the whole of England and Wales though not at present Scotland. A number of Harvey 1:25 000 walkers' maps are also available. Maps are sold on CD-ROM and DVD. In addition Anquet has made Ordnance Survey digital mapping available online. The walker is able to define the area and scale of the map they want, chosen from Explorer or Landranger maps, and download it to their PC together with aerial photography if required. This is a fast-moving market and products will change but this gives an idea of what is currently available.

Of course, some people will use this mapping without combining it with a gps, but for gps users it makes life much easier and more interesting. On the computer screen Ordnance Survey maps come into their own and you can really appreciate them in full colour glory. Definition and detail is clear, making them a pleasure to view and use. The 'Find' function enables a quick search to locate either a grid reference or place name. Sections of the map you are planning to walk can be printed off

Anquet's virtual landscape

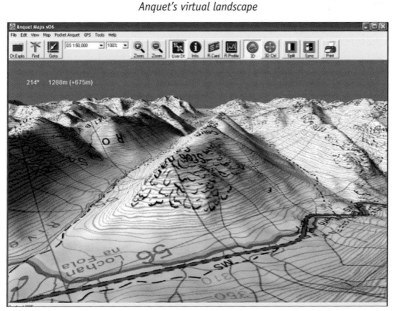

in full colour for use in the field: so convenient and easy to refer to.

You experience the full power of Anquet software when it comes to creating waypoints, routes or tracks. For example, if you are planning a walk you call up the relevant map on your PC screen and, using your mouse, click out your proposed route. You can access all sorts of data about your route: its length, estimated walking time, waypoint information such as compass bearings, altitude, grid references and a graph showing the route profile. Notes can be included and route cards created, all much easier and more informative than doing things manually.

Another exciting feature is Anquet's virtual landscape (see page 53). You can see your route cross the contoured landscape in 3-D, even more impressive when you switch to aerial photography. The 'Fly Over' function allows you to travel your planned route with a bird's eye view of the ground to be walked. The screen can be split with the 3-D map on one side and you 'flying over' your path on the other. Using the virtual landscape is excellent for pre-planning a walk especially if it is to be in difficult terrain. You can get a real picture of what you are about to undertake and a mental image you can carry with you, valuable if you encounter very bad weather.

When your planning and virtual travelling is complete you can transfer the route, track or waypoint data to your gps in an instant. It could not be easier. Then on completion of your walk your tracklog can be transferred to your computer and you can see exactly where you have walked and compare it with the route you planned. Your data can be manipulated in various ways, for example you could turn it into a route or re-walk it in virtual reality using the virtual landscape. You can then switch to the high definition aerial photograph and see your path traced out on the ground. Photo maps can be used on their own or linked to any Anquet map. Routes, tracks and waypoints can be created using photo maps in the same way as with the digital Ordnance Survey maps.

Also it is possible to load Anquet maps to your pocket PC if you have one, permitting you to see where you are at a given moment ('real time live positioning') and follow your progress on uploaded Ordnance Survey maps. You can create routes and carry out similar tasks as on your desktop PC but with the advantage of portability.

Anquet software is also compatible with Microsoft enabled Smart-phones allowing you to use them for navigation when used with, for example, a screenless gps receiver (e.g. a Bluetooth enabled gps), probably more suited to urban direction finding than for walkers out on the hill.

The Anquet 'virtual gps' feature replicates the functions of a standard gps receiver so that you can use a screenless gps receiver (usually less expensive) and get the same information on your laptop, pocket PC or Smartphone. You get a similar directional arrow and compass ring to guide you just as on your eTrex or other standard gps.

The Anquet software is easy to use after you have familiarised yourself with the details of the program. It is flexible and allows you to customise many functions to suit your needs. Anquet has a lively website where you can find periodic updates for your software, exchange routes with other walkers and download walks from sources such as *Trail* and *Country Walking* magazines.

An example of a stand-alone program available on the Internet

'GPS Utility is a stand-alone application for managing, manipulating and mapping waypoints, route and trackpoint information' (GPSU).

This is a program developed in the UK and is available on the Internet as both a Freeware (free of charge) and a fuller Shareware version (currently costing £30). The Freeware program which you can download in a few minutes allows the scanning of a section of map, the creation of 100 waypoints, five routes of up to ten waypoints each and 500 trackpoints: sufficient features for you to explore and use the program and make up your own mind about it. It is popular with gps users and has a dedicated following.

In brief, the software enables you to transfer data between your gps and PC. Amongst the things you can do are to create waypoints, routes and tracks; do all sorts of data editing and analysis; turn tracks into routes and vice versa; exchange data with other programs (e.g. you can view walks in Google Earth); convert between different map datums and many co-ordinate formats and use scanned-in maps to record and plot gps information. It is also possible to create your own maps. You can scan in portions of foreign maps as well as Ordnance Survey maps (be aware of copyright issues). Once you have acquired the necessary skills and requisite map information to 'calibrate' your scanned-in map, you can pre-plan your routes at home and transfer your walks to your gps receiver for use at home and abroad.

A basic use of the program is to type in a list of grid references read off your paper map and upload them to your gps. This is much easier than doing it manually and reduces the possibility of error. You will find this function simple to use. The program has many layers and features and enables you to do a great many things with your data. You can use it with most makes and models of gps. It does take some time and effort to come to terms with its more advanced functions. A detailed 'Help' menu gives a full description of functions and guides you in their use. At first, go especially to the tutorial 'Getting Started with GPS Utility' at **www.gpsu.co.uk/tutorial/** or via the Help/Tutorial in GPSU. The more computer-literate you are the quicker you will pick things up. It is well worth persevering because you will enjoy and appreciate the results. Have a look at the GPSU website yourself: **www.gpsu.co.uk**

GPS Utility is used by several organisations involved in providing emergency relief throughout the world. Emergency workers who are not trained land surveyors can still use a consumer grade gps receiver to quickly gather geographic data regarding emergency situations (earthquakes, tsunami, floods, etc.). By using GPS Utility they can then very quickly produce maps and information which is useful to relief planning and to other members of the emergency team. Oxfam used GPSU in the Sudan and the Asian tsunami for water and sanitation planning. The program was also used in New Orleans to help locate pets after Hurricane Katrina.

Planning a high level route: the Newlands Horseshoe

The Newlands Horseshoe walk is taken from *Pathfinder 22 More Lake District Walks*, walk 24 (see map on page 61, top right). The Newlands Horseshoe is one of the finest ridge walks in the Lakes and is about 13.7 kilometres (8½ miles) long and takes about 5½ hours to walk. You take in four summits and on a clear day the views are spectacular but *it is no place to be in bad conditions unless you are an experienced fell walker*. What follows are some ways the planning may be approached.

1 Planning the walk without using a computer

As you know, you can use a gps on your walk without getting involved in computers and gps software. You can collect the references that make up your route and enter them into your gps manually. Your co-ordinates can be taken from a map, guidebook, the Internet or other source but it is easier to use a PC, which considerably expands your range of possibilities.

2 Software programs produced by gps manufacturers

You can use a gps with mapping capability together with the manufacturers' software. For example, Garmin sell their Topo Great Britain *based* on Ordnance Survey mapping for use on their gps. The

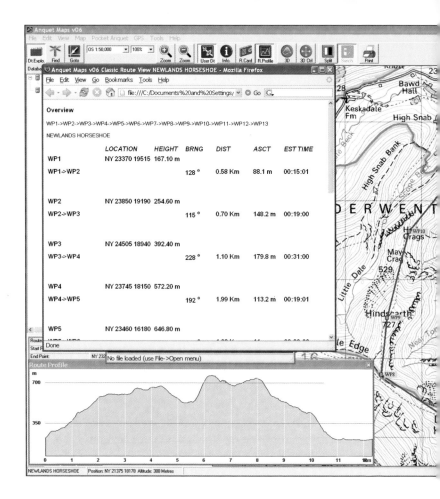

map is transferred to your gps via your computer and your route appears on the gps screen together with your pointer and other navigational information.

The Ordnance Survey-based maps Garmin produce to use with their gps (see page 57)

3 Software produced by a digital mapping company

The illustration (above) shows the Newlands Horseshoe route with its waypoints. A section of route card and route profile are included to illustrate the kind of information the software will generate (insets, top left). You just click out your route with your cursor

creating the number of waypoints you require which can then be transferred into your gps. It could not be easier. The two other illustrations (below) display the route in 3-D showing the contours and the configuration of a part of the Newlands Valley and surrounding mountains together with an aerial photograph. You are able to explore and see the whole map in this way. One of the advantages of the program is that you can walk your route in virtual reality before setting out and get a real picture of your walk which might stand you in good stead should the weather turn against you. In any case it makes your progress along your path more relaxing because you carry a mental picture of your route. On returning home you can transfer your tracklog and see where you actually walked and how it relates to your planned route. There are programs other than Anquet that use Ordnance Survey mapping and do a very similar job, for example Memory-Map.

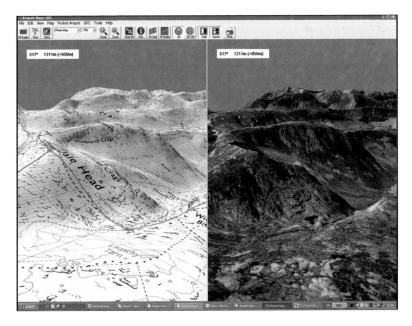

4 A stand-alone program available on the Internet

This is an example of a planned and walked route of the Newlands Horseshoe. The screen shot shows numbered waypoints and co-ordinates which were taken from a paper map and entered into the GPSU software before being transferred to a gps. On the right there is a map showing the route with its distribution of waypoints. The Report window (bottom) shows the waypoint co-ordinates, bearing and distance to the next waypoint.

GPS Utility (4.20.4)

File GPS Record View Tools Options Window Help

Newlands Horseshoe4a.txt - Waypoints

(13) Info. British grid ▼ Ord Srvy Gr

ID	Coordinate	Symbol	T	O	Comment
W001	NY 23370 19515	Waypoint	I	NW	
W002	NY 23850 19190	Waypoint	I	NE	
W003	NY 24505 18940	Waypoint	I	E	
W004	NY 23745 18150	Waypoint	I	W	
W005	NY 23460 16180	Waypoint	I	E	
W006	NY 23060 15163	Waypoint	I	SE	
W007	NY 22305 15250	Waypoint	I	SW	
W008	NY 21465 15795	Waypoint	I	NE	
W009	NY 21545 16515	Waypoint	I	NW	
W010	NY 21835 17610	Waypoint	I	W	
W011	NY 22750 18710	Waypoint	I	NW	
W012	NY 23035 18050	Waypoint	I	S	
W013	NY 23210 19170	Waypoint	I	NW	

GPS Utility Report

SaveAs... Print Copy View Options Close Help

Route Information ▼   Route: 1: Newlands Horseshoe

Route number	1
Route name	Newlands Horseshoe
Number of waypoints	13
Route Distance(km)	12.362

ID	Coordinate	Degs	Dist(km)
W001	NY 23370 19515	124	0.580
W002	NY 23850 19190	111	0.701
W003	NY 24505 18940	224	1.096
W004	NY 23745 18150	188	1.991
W005	NY 23460 16180	201	1.093
W006	NY 23060 15163	277	0.760
W007	NY 22305 15250	303	1.001
W008	NY 21465 15795	006	0.724
W009	NY 21545 16515	015	1.133
W010	NY 21835 17610	040	1.431
W011	NY 22750 18710	157	0.719
W012	NY 23035 18050	009	1.134
W013	NY 23210 19170		

End to Start(km)	0.380
Area enclosed(hectares)	644.892

After the walk the tracklog was transferred into the GPSU program which provided a schematic map of the tracklog together with other data relating to the walk. This walked tracklog is shown in blue and you can see how it relates to the planned route (green).

The tracklog illustrates that where you walk is not necessarily exactly the same as your planned route. Your gps indicates waypoint to waypoint in straight lines which is not how we walk. Paths on the map which you use for your planning are usually rights of way and do not necessarily correspond exactly to the actual paths on the ground: aerial photographs can show this very clearly. Some of the very obvious departures from the route were a combination of avoiding dangerous areas of ice and snow and seeking a good position to photograph the spectacular winter scenes. The map scale you are using to plan your walk needs to be borne in mind: Ordnance Survey 1:50 000 Landranger (good for reading the contours) are less detailed than the 1:25 000 Explorer maps. Also satellite reception varies as we have seen.

If you are a more advanced user you can scan in a section of map and see information relating to your walk set out on it. You can create

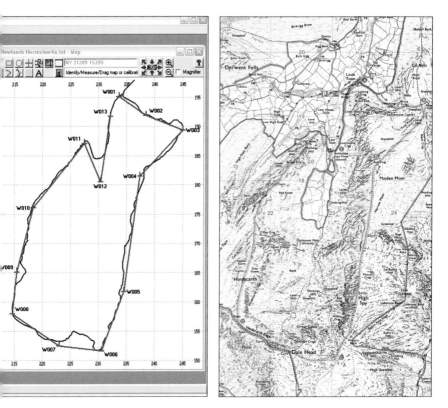

your waypoints, route or tracklog (before walking your path if you wish) on this digitised map and use 'tracklog navigation' to complete it. You can go on to work with your data in various ways and you can use it to fly over your route in Google Earth.

The last leg of the Newlands Horseshoe

Walking guides and gps

Walking is one of the UK's most popular leisure activities. A wealth of walking publications is available covering most areas of the country. Usually they have descriptions of local walks graded in terms of difficulty and time. The better guides include sections of Ordnance Survey maps with the walks outlined. More often there will be just a sketch map.

Many walking guides and maps are now beginning to be 'gps enabled' which means a list of waypoints is included alongside the walk's description. GPS waypoint co-ordinates are being included in Jarrold's *Pathfinder* and *Short Walks* guides as part of the regular updates to the series, to enable you to enjoy the full benefits of gps.

Your gps gives an added dimension. The advantage of using a gps is that it introduces 'direction' into your walking which can be lacking in verbal instructions alone. Also you are able to take in the environment more because you do not need to concentrate on the book so much. Use of a gps brings greater confidence and security to your walking and you can cover ground a lot faster should you need to.

The walk shown opposite is an example of using a gps on a walk in the south of the UK. Navigation in the lowland areas can be as challenging as in the upland areas but in a different way. For example, paths can be quite intricate and sometimes finding the beginning of the walk can take a while. Using a gps can smooth your way and minimise those puzzling moments when you are not quite sure whether it is this way or that.

Pathfinder Kent, Walk 20
Thurnham and Hollingbourne

Start	Cobham Manor Riding Centre, Thurnham
Distance	7½ miles (12km)
Approximate time	4 hours
Parking	Car park at Cobham Manor Riding Centre
Refreshments	Coffee shop at Cobham Manor Riding Centre, pubs at Thurnham and Hollingbourne
Ordnance Survey maps	Landranger 178, Explorer 148

GPS waypoints

🖉	TQ 81590 57300
Ⓐ	TQ 80810 58010
Ⓑ	TQ 82480 57570
Ⓒ	TQ 84130 56690
Ⓓ	TQ 82640 56260
Ⓔ	TQ 82200 56980

Geocaching – a gps treasure hunt

This rather strange looking word refers to a relatively new high-tech treasure hunt. Geocaching, pronounced geo-khash-ing, is derived from the 'geo' of geography and 'cache', a hiding place. The game grew out of the increasing popularity of both gps receivers and the Internet.

The pastime resembles the older treasure hunt of 'letterboxing' which many British walkers may know as it originated on Dartmoor and became very popular. In letterboxing the treasure hunt is driven by clues. The hunt involves finding a waterproof letterbox which contains a logbook and rubber stamp. When it is found the person stamps or signs the logbook and marks their own log with the stamp found in the box.

Geocaching was launched in America by a gps user who wanted to celebrate President Clinton's decision to switch off Selective Availability in May 2000, thereby greatly improving the accuracy of civilian gps receivers at a stroke. He hid a bucket containing trinkets and a logbook in a wood and posted the co-ordinates of its location (waypoint) on the Internet, inviting others to find it. The sport of geocaching was born and grew with remarkable speed.

At its most basic the game is played along the following lines. Some-one (family, group or organisation) hides a waterproof container. It

On the trail of the cache

can be hidden anywhere. Its waypoint co-ordinates are recorded by gps and posted on the web. Typically, inside the container there will be a logbook and perhaps some other item(s) included by the cache's creator. The seeker will then enter the co-ordinates into his/her gps and set off to hunt the container down. The rules are that when it is found the finder should make an entry in the logbook and hopefully leave something for the next person in order to keep the game going. Finally the finder should report back to the website where he/she originally got details of the cache.

Geocaching is surprisingly popular and is played by individuals and groups worldwide. All you need to take part is a basic gps, access to the Internet and pleasure in the chase. The game has evolved greatly over its short life. Caches and finding them have become ever more creative and sophisticated. However, the essentials of the game remain the same: to use your gps in a fun way. Gps manufacturers are now including geocaching features on their units.

> *The most popular and informative source of information on geocaching and details of caches is found at: www.geocaching.com*

There is a Geocaching Association of Great Britain (GAGB) but the most popular and informative source of information on geocaching and details of caches is found at: www.geocaching.com. This is by far the best place to look if you wish to learn more about geocaching or take part in it yourself.

Checking the location

Handheld computers, PDAs and Smartphones

Handheld computers or PDAs (Personal Digital Assistants) are pocket-sized PCs. There is a bewildering number on the market with different specifications and prices. We will refer to these generally and discuss only those units that use Microsoft Windows software. PDAs run mini versions of popular programs like Microsoft Pocket Office that includes Pocket Outlook, Pocket Word, Pocket Excel. You can carry out other functions such as storing photographs or listening to music. They can be bought bundled with navigation software and are popular with motorists for in-car navigation. PDAs are easily linked to your laptop or desktop PC allowing you to exchange data and sections of mapping.

For the purpose of navigation for walkers we can divide pocket PCs into those that have an integrated gps and those that do not. If a PDA does not have a built-in gps you can then either attach a standard gps to it with a lead or perhaps use a screenless gps with Bluetooth (wireless) with a Bluetooth-enabled PDA. This removes the necessity for leads and makes it more practical outdoors. An advantage of using a Bluetooth gps is that you have two sources of power. Most Bluetooth gps use standard phone batteries, so spares are not too difficult to come by. PDAs tend to use their own batteries: you can sometimes get spare rechargeable batteries but they are neither cheap nor as readily available.

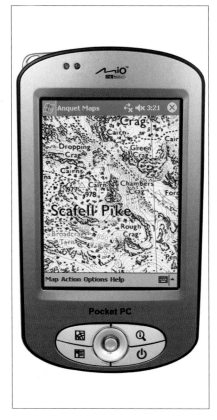

The great advantages of handheld PCs over standard gps lie mainly in their larger clearer colour screens and the range of digital maps and other software available. A very big advantage is that unlike standard gps receivers you are not tied into the maps of an individual gps manufacturer. For example, you can use the maps produced by Anquet, Memory-Map or other companies. Expandable memory capacity is a further plus point. Pocket computers are very portable so you can use them on the move to see your current location (real time positioning) and progress along your route on maps uploaded from your laptop or desktop.

Mio P350

However, for walkers all these advantages may be outweighed by some severe disadvantages when compared with a standard gps. Above all, affordable models are not yet suited to the outdoors. They will not take as much punishment as a standard gps. They are not waterproof and many, although not all, have fitted rechargeable batteries that last only a few hours and need to be charged from a power source. Protective covers are available which afford some protection against the elements but these can be clumsy to use in the field. No doubt manufacturers will come up with answers to these problems in the not too distant future.

There is a great deal of information available on the Internet and you would be well advised to consult it before buying because PDAs are not cheap. However, prices are falling steadily and they are becoming much more affordable. A good place to start your research is the website www.gpsinformation.net and in particular the writings of Dale De Priest who covers every angle you could possibly think of and more.

Smartphones

Since the development and widespread ownership of mobile telephones, they have become an integral part of modern life. There are many more Smartphones than PDAs and exciting developments in navigation are taking place here as well. Smartphone 'functionality' is similar to that of PDAs. You can view digital maps and plan routes on them that you can navigate using Anquet software that is compatible with Microsoft-enabled Smartphones. You could link your Smartphone to a screenless gps using Bluetooth (wireless) technology, although Smartphones with gps built in are now available.

i-mate Smartphone

With Anquet's Virtual GPS, a feature of their mapping, you can get the same information on your PDA/Smartphone screen as is shown on your gps screen, e.g. a directional arrow and information on the next waypoint. It is probably true to say that developments in Smartphones are likely to be of more use to walkers in the city than in the countryside but they could be of use to both. Like PDAs they are not yet as rugged as a standard gps.

Suunto X9i

Wrist watches with gps are now available e.g. the Suunto X9i which has an integral 12 channel gps, compass, altimeter and barometer. You can create waypoints, routes and tracks. It has a number of grids and datums and connects to a PC, which allows you to 'use Suunto Trek Manager or numerous different companies' software for planning and reviewing your hikes' (Suunto).

Useful hints on using a gps

Agps and computer are highly sophisticated electronic devices that are subject to all sorts of complex issues beyond the scope of this book but it may be useful to look at one or two practical points, some of which may cause you to scratch your head early in your gps-walking career.

1 Practise using your gps

It is a good idea to get to know your gps and its foibles before you use it for real. Walk around your neighbourhood with it. Create some waypoints and use the GOTO function. Put together a short route and follow it. Go under some trees and look at how the signal strength is affected.

2 Paper maps

Your gps is complementary to your other navigational skills. It is a great addition but always take the relevant paper map covering your walk. During your walk periodically take grid references from your gps to check your progress on the map. Navigation experts teach that you should know approximately where you are at any given moment. Mountain rescue team leaders advise that most accidents are caused by poor navigation.

3 Before setting out on a walk

Save or delete any previous tracklogs. Clear your track memory. Reset the trip metres. Use your paper map to orientate yourself before you start walking. Your gps will soon start to guide you but you will need to be moving.

4 Check your batteries and carry spares

Check your batteries. If you have not used your receiver for a while it is likely that your batteries will need recharging if using rechargeables. Make sure you carry a set of spare batteries. To be on the safe side do always carry some spare rechargeable batteries together with a set of Duracell ones. Rechargeable batteries can be temperamental.

5 My gps will not work

One of the main reasons you may not get any response from your receiver after you switch it on may be to do with the batteries. Rechargeable batteries lose their charge over time. It is good practice to always check your batteries before setting out.

Do the batteries fit badly and not make good contact? Different makes of AA/AAA batteries can vary in diameter. Wedging them with a scrap of paper can solve this problem.

Are your battery contacts clean? Have you put them in the right way round? If you have not used your gps for some time, or if you have travelled some distance from where you last used it, your receiver may take a while to update its data, i.e. a cold start.

Check satellite reception

6 I cannot get any reception on my gps

Are you indoors? Your gps will not work inside any buildings unless you happen to be near a window and are very lucky. Is there something obstructing the satellite signal? Are you under trees? Is your own body in the way? Are you in a ravine? Is there a mountain in the way? Your gps will work in your car if there is nothing in the make-up of your windscreen to interfere with your reception.

If you are going to enter tree cover make sure you have a strong reception before you enter the wood as you are then more likely to get some response under the trees, but it's a little hit or miss. Look for a clearing in the trees where you may be able to pick up a signal.

7 Are you walking in the right direction?

Some gps offer you the choice of which way round you wish to walk your saved tracklog or route. The options seem clear enough on your gps but concentrate before making your choice. Make a practice of checking your first waypoint.

Also remember that your gps can sometimes lock onto the nearest or next waypoint. It may override the one you think you are heading for. For example, at the beginning of a circular day's walk it could fix on a waypoint on the return leg of your walk.

At a junction, if you are not quite sure of your way, just choose the direction you think is right. Your gps direction arrow will point you back if it is incorrect and you can now proceed along the correct path.

8 I am getting odd gps readings which I know to be wrong

Check that you are using the correct datum and grid system appropriate to the map you are using. You will need to go into your gps set-up to do this.

9 My gps compass readings do not quite correspond with my map

Remember if you want your gps to agree with your map you need to select grid north in the set-up on your gps receiver. If you want to use your compass with your gps select magnetic north.

10 I am using latitude and longitude on my gps but it does not match with this lat/long reference

There are three ways of expressing a location in latitude or longitude. The most common of these is the hddd.mm.mmm format, but there are two other formats and they do look very different (see page 86). You may find these three ways quite confusing.

11 Can I use my gps in all weathers?

Yes. Most gps are quite waterproof and reasonably rugged: you will find specific details of just how waterproof in your manual. A drop of rain will not hurt them but sometimes they do have a vulnerable spot. On the eTrex it is the battery compartment. If you use it in a downpour just take the batteries out and wipe it dry on your return home. For all practical purposes your gps will not be affected by the weather.

12 How can I protect my gps?

There are plenty of different carrying cases on the market designed for receivers. Garmin produce a handy case and carrying loop that provides protection for the unit but in wet or humid weather the plastic window can cloud over and make it difficult to read. There are other makes of plastic pouch-like covers that you can buy in outdoor shops.

13 How and where can I carry my gps?

One issue that may arise when using your gps is how and where to carry it, especially if you use two walking poles. Additionally the occasional use of a compass and map can make things quite difficult: there are just not enough hands. Try attaching your gps high up on the straps of your rucksack where it has a good view of the sky. Carrying your gps on your belt or hanging it around your neck reduces the accuracy of readings owing to the obstruction of your body, known as 'body shadowing'.

14 I cannot seem to get my gps to communicate with my computer

If you are trying to get your gps to transfer data to your PC and are having no success then two useful things to check are:

- The COM port. Are you using the correct COM port on your computer, i.e. a COM port that is not used by another accessory like your mouse or printer?

- If you are using a USB lead, have you installed the driver for it? You will probably find it on the accompanying CD.

Also, check that any leads you are using are properly inserted and driven home, a very common source of problems.

15 Do not be controlled by your gps

Do not keep looking at your gps. You are walking to enjoy yourself and relax. Apart from the danger of falling over, it will detract from your enjoyment of your surroundings. You could transfer a route into your gps then not refer to it, using the map or your own knowledge of the walk instead. Meanwhile your gps is ready and waiting for you should you run into bad weather or a difficult piece of route-finding.

Your gps is a wonderful piece of technology but is a means to an end, not an end in itself. Keep your wits about you and your eye on the map, and don't forget to look at the view.

Buying a gps receiver

There are two main manufacturers of gps readily available on the high street: Garmin and Magellan. It is difficult to recommend specific units as the best buy owing to personal preference, ever-changing choice and need. You may wish to begin with an entry-level gps owing to its ease of use but new products are coming onto the market all the time and are increasingly aimed at specific users. You will find more choice, lower prices and better information on the Internet than in the shops.

Most gps receivers on sale will do a perfectly adequate job and have very similar specifications but it may be useful to set out some general criteria to bear in mind when buying.

- Keep it simple. As with most modern technology one can go on adding features – at a cost. Do you really need all those extra functions? Out on the hill in adverse weather conditions, easy access to basic information is all-important.

- Can you read the screen easily? Imagine being in bad weather.

- Look at battery life. The longer it is the fewer spares you will need to carry. All those extra functions, like an electronic compass, can be heavy on your batteries.

| Magellan eXplorist 500 | Magellan eXplorist 600 | Magellan eXplorist XL |

- The function: 'bearing to next waypoint' is characteristic of most units but is particularly important for walking.

- Get a unit capable of storing at least 20 routes and 500 waypoints.

- You should get at least a 12-channel parallel receiver for best reception (almost standard now).

- Most gps have a good selection of datums and grid systems but make sure the areas you want to walk in are included.

- Built-in maps are a nice feature but not essential. They can help in locating you although they are not very detailed or necessarily accurate. A memory of at least 32MB or more is desirable in a mapping unit. As a general principle, the greater the memory, the better. Some receivers have expandable memory because they use memory cards. Remember, receivers with mapping capability work only with maps produced by the manufacturer, e.g. Garmin receivers will only accept Garmin's *MapSource* and no Magellan map products or those of any other manufacturer.

- Computer interface (connection). Ability to communicate with a PC enables the transfer of waypoints, tracks and routes between the two. At the time of purchase you may not be interested in this but who knows how your interests will develop?

- Portable and waterproof. You need to be able to carry your unit and refer to it easily in all weathers, (a limitation of PDAs or hand-held computers).

- It is now wise to buy a receiver with WAAS and EGNOS in preparation for when these systems come into full use.

- Increasingly manufacturers are using USB connections owing to their faster transmission of data to and from a computer. At the time of writing many receivers use a serial connection to the PC. Makers of laptop computers are increasingly omitting a serial connection in their products, meaning a gps with a serial connection will not communicate with the latest laptops without additional hardware, so make sure you buy a laptop/gps that are compatible.

A good way of checking out whether a particular receiver is what you want is to go to the manufacturer's website and download the manuals which are available online and check out the features. A lot of information is available on the Internet and is usually of more help than that available in most retail shops.

Garmin geko 201   *Garmin eTrex Vista 60CX*   *Garmin GPSmap 60CSx*

Working with Ordnance Survey maps: grid references

G rid references enable you to refer to a precise point on a map and to communicate it to others should you need to. In the UK, Ordnance Survey uses the British National Grid Reference System which overlays a grid of squares on the map of the British Isles.

> Grid references enable you to refer to a precise point on a map and to communicate it to others should you need to.

Squares of 100 by 100 kilometres, which have been given a two-letter prefix, are further sub-divided into 1 kilometre squares.

The Ordnance Survey Landranger (1:50 000 scale) and the Explorer (1:25 000 scale) maps are divided into kilometre squares by faint blue lines: those running North/South are called 'Eastings' because their numbers run eastwards, while those running East/West are referred to as 'Northings,' as they are numbered northwards on your map. Look at an Ordnance Survey map and you will see what we mean. Easting numbers are always given before Northings. One way to remember this is that E comes before N in the alphabet. The squares on 1:50 000 maps are 2cm and those on 1:25 000 maps are 4cm. On both, the distance from side to side represents 1 kilometre on the ground. The diagonal between the square's corners represents roughly $1\frac{1}{2}$ kilometres on the ground.

Within each 100 kilometre square, the blue lines on the map are numbered 00–99 in each direction. References or co-ordinates always start with the Easting first, followed by the Northing, so in a six-figure grid reference the first three figures show how far east a point is while the last three figures tell us how far north it is in the square. In the grid reference on page 80, 215 is the Easting and 072 the Northing.

Each kilometre square is delineated by two numbers that are read off the map. In our example they are 21 and 07. Now imagine the kilometre square divided into tenths, so these are numbered 1 to 10 up the vertical and along the horizontal axes of the square, dividing the kilometre square notionally into 10 by 10, 100 metre squares. You can estimate the third and sixth figure (5 and 2) of the grid reference in tenths of the square to locate the point more precisely. If you went to the grid reference in the example (see over) you would find yourself standing on the highest part of England: Scafell Pike.

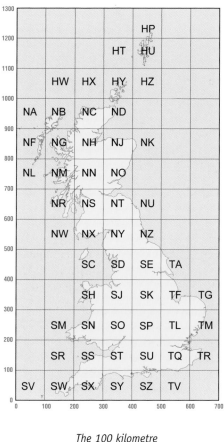

The 100 kilometre squares with identifying letters

The two letters preceding the numbers should be used in grid references in order to prevent confusion. Grid lines (blue lines) on Ordnance Survey maps are numbered 00–99. Six-figure references are thus repeated every 100 kilometres (62 miles) across the National Grid Reference System and so we need a system for distinguishing them. In the following example the letters NY indicate the particular 100-kilometre square your map falls in. In practice, these letters are often omitted but when you are inputting co-ordinates into your gps you must include them. You will find the two letters relevant to the location in question written in the legend on the Ordnance Survey map you are using.

One of the most valuable functions of your gps is to give the grid reference of a given location. The eTrex provides a 10-figure reference for UK maps but for most purposes a six-figure location is good enough. Take the first three numbers of each of the two sets of numbers of the 10-figure readout to get the six-figure grid reference.

For example, on your gps the location of Scafell Pike would appear as follows:

NY **215**40
BNG **072**11

(BNG = British National Grid and is not part of the reference)

The six-figure reference is: NY **215072**

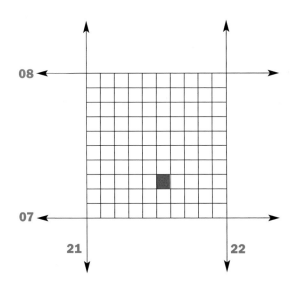

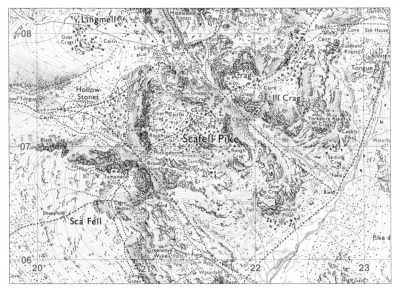

A six-figure grid reference refers to a 100 metre square (i.e. an area), marked in red in the diagram (more accurately the SW corner of the square), worth remembering when using your gps to locate yourself. An eight-figure reference locates a point within a 10-metre square (100 metre square further divided into 10 x 10 metre squares). Here you take the first four figures of the two groupings of numbers on your gps readout: NY 21540721. A 10-figure reference locates you within one metre. For most walkers a six-figure reference should be sufficient. To enter a six-figure (215072) reference into your gps you can add '00' to each pair of co-ordinates e.g. NY 21500 07200.

A Romer

Using a 'romer' helps to pinpoint a location using a map reference like the one previously. You can buy a romer or make one yourself. Some compasses have romers marked out on their base plates. You use them to accurately count out the location of the reference within the kilometre map square.

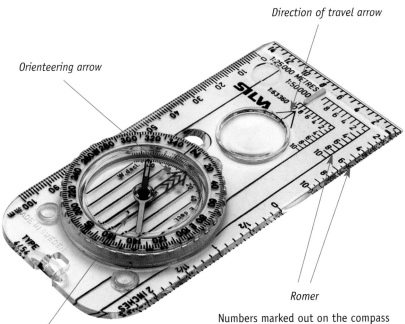

Direction of travel arrow

Orienteering arrow

N/S lines

Romer

Numbers marked out on the compass to count off tenths of kilometre for different map scales.

Gps and your compass

Taking a bearing with map and compass

1. Place the compass on map with edge along desired line of travel. Make sure Direction of Travel arrow points towards your destination.

2. Rotate capsule until N on graduation ring point towards North on the map. Check compass housing North/South lines are parallel to map meridians.

3. Hold compass horizontally in front of you. Turn yourself until red end of the needle points towards N on the compass graduation ring. (Red end of needle will now be aligned to red North arrow in bottom of the compass capsule.) Direction of Travel arrow now points precisely to your destination. Look up, sight on a land-mark and walk to it. Repeat this procedure until you reach your destination.

Text copyright The Silva 1-2-3 System © Silva

A very useful skill for walkers is to know how to use your compass to take a bearing from your map to where you want to go. The Silva 1-2-3 System shows how you do this in three simple stages using a compass with a base plate. The compass will give you your bearing. It is important to remember grid north, magnetic north and magnetic variation mentioned before which will mean an adjustment to your bearing before you follow it. If you

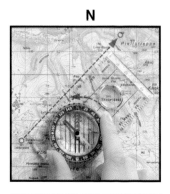

N

take a bearing from a map to be used with a compass, as in the illustration, you have to add the magnetic variation, whereas if you have taken a bearing with your compass in the field to be used on your paper map you have to subtract it (in Britain). Remember: 'Add for mag, get rid for grid'.

Your compass bearing will be a straight line direction to your destination and just as when you are moving waypoint to waypoint using your gps, you need to be cautious of potential obstacles and dangers in your path. There are a number of techniques you can use to ensure accuracy and safety

Go into 'Set Up' to set your gps to give you magnetic and grid north. Magnetic variation will change as you travel around the world.

while walking on a compass bearing. If you would like to know more about this absorbing subject a good place to start is to get hold of the free pamphlets on map reading and navigation published by Ordnance Survey.

When you are stationary your gps (unless it has an electronic compass) will not give you directional information whereas a compass will. You can use your compass in partnership with your gps. For example, on a long hike you could take the bearing from your gps to the next waypoint and transfer it to your compass and follow it as in Step 3 in the Silva 1-2-3 System. This could be useful where you are very low on battery power (because you can turn your gps off) or where you are going to enter very dense tree cover and possibly lose your signal. Remember: set your gps to magnetic north and the bearing it gives will correspond to your compass. Set your gps to grid north and it will correspond to the bearing taken from your map as in the illustration.

The Silva 1-2-3 system

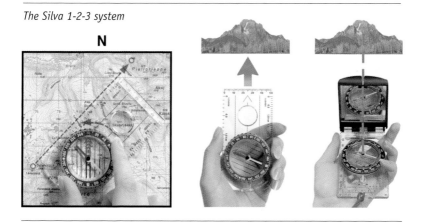

You can experiment on your gps by changing between grid and magnetic north and seeing the bearing it gives you for a selected waypoint. The bearing number may change but not the direction. On a challenging walk it is good practice to carry a paper map and compass with you and to know how to use them.

Using your gps abroad

You may well want to do some of your walking abroad. If you do not know already you will soon discover that not all foreign maps are as easy to use as Ordnance Survey maps. You will in all probability have to come to terms with different map co-ordinate (grid) systems. The two most useful and widely used are latitude and longitude, and the easier to use UTM (Universal Transverse Mercator System). To find out more about these systems see the list of resources in the bibliography. A helpful diagram of UTM can be found at: www.dmap.co.uk/utmworld.htm.

> *Change to the datum relevant to the map and country of your walking area. Choose a position format (grid system).*

You must adjust the settings in your *gps set-up*. The first thing to do is to check the local map to see if there are any grid reference systems and map datums specified. If there are, then use those.

- Change to the *datum* relevant to the map of your walking area.
- Choose a *position format (grid system)*.

When you choose a position format from the list given in the eTrex it will automatically select an appropriate datum for many locations.

- Select the relevant *time zone*.

1 Latitude and longitude

The default grid system (position format) on Garmin receivers is latitude and longitude.

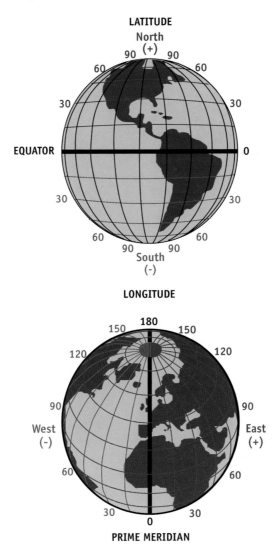

Imaginary grid lines are drawn over the Earth's surface. Latitude lines run parallel to the equator, the equator being designated 0 degrees. The North Pole is 90 degrees N and the South Pole 90 degrees S. Lines of longitude called meridians radiate from the N Pole to the S Pole. The prime meridian passing through Greenwich in London is 0 degrees and the lines of longitude run E to 180 degrees and W to 180 degrees.

To enable precise location using this grid system the degrees of latitude and longitude are further sub-divided into 'minutes' and 'seconds' which relate to the geometry of a circle (360 degrees) rather than time. So:

- One degree of *latitude* is divided into 60' minutes and one minute into 60" seconds.

- One degree of *longitude* is also divided into 60' minutes and one minute into 60" seconds.

Note: *the signs used to denote minutes ' and seconds ".*

A grid reference using this system is written with *latitude first,* e.g. **N 54° 27' 14.7" and W003° 12' 37.1"** (Scafell Pike: OSGB datum). Ordnance Survey maps have latitude and longitude co-ordinates clearly written along the margins of their maps enabling the use of this grid system. Unfortunately not all foreign maps are as helpful and so it is not always as easy to use them.

Latitude and longitude is complicated by the fact that there are three ways of expressing a given location using latitude and longitude. Your receiver should have all three formats. Modern receivers make it easy to convert between them and indeed between different grid systems. It is an interesting thing to do just to see the different ways of expressing the same location. Below are the three ways of expressing a reference (Scafell Pike) in latitude and longitude.

1. Hemisphere degrees: hddd.ddddd:
N 54.45408° W 003.21032°

2. Hemisphere degrees minutes: hddd.mm.mmm:
N 54° 27.245' W 003° 12.619'

3. Hemisphere degree minutes, seconds: hddd mm ss.s:
N 54° 27' 14.7" W 003° 12' 37.1"

The Ordnance Survey equivalent 10-figure reference for this location is NY 21540 07211.

The most used method is *degree minutes* of latitude and longitude hddd.mm.mmm.

Your gps will convert between these different latitude and longitude formats should you need to. Also you can further convert these into UTM/OS co-ordinates on your receiver.

Most maps will have latitude and longitude scales running along their edges. (Their ease of use depends on how helpful the map-maker has been.) You read off the latitude first, which runs horizontally and can be read off along the sides of the map, dividing the latitude minutes into seconds. Half a minute will be 30 seconds and so on. The same is done for longitude meridians

Using a gps in Mallorca

that run vertically and are read off along the top and bottom of the map, so you get a latitude and longitude reading to locate the position on the map in the same manner as you would with any grid reference system like the more familiar Ordnance Survey grid.

Publishers of foreign maps and guidebooks are beginning to make the walker's life a bit easier by making maps 'gps enabled', including lists of waypoints with their co-ordinates to accompany paths and route descriptions. You can enter these into your receiver.

Entering latitude and longitude into your gps

You input the latitude and longitude co-ordinates into your gps just as you would Ordnance Survey references but in one of the three formats of latitude and longitude you will have previously selected in your gps set-up. Use whichever format is most convenient for you. This may depend upon the map you are using.

Choose (for instance) *hddd.mm.mmm* from the position format list in your 'set-up' option and enter the co-ordinates into your gps as you would an Ordnance Survey reference. You will have to include the N and W followed by the relevant numbers, e.g. N 54° 27 245' W 003° 12. 619' for Scafell Pike.

2 Universal Transverse Mercator Grid (UTM)

The second grid system that you may come across is UTM. It is much easier to use than latitude and longitude especially as it closely resembles the Ordnance Survey grid reference system. The system grew out of the needs of the military and is now used by the US army and NATO but it is also found on many foreign maps, often alongside the latitude and longitude grid system.

The basis of the UTM grid system is a division of the world into 60 zones running north and south, each six degrees of longitude wide, with each of these zones wrapping around the Earth's surface starting at 180 W and numbering 1 to 60 eastwards: these are called the Eastings. Measurements are given in metres from the zone's baseline.

The Northings are formed by 20 bands, eight degrees wide moving out north and south from the equator to latitude 84 degrees north and 80 degrees south and also describe distance in metres from the equator. Northings are each assigned a letter of the alphabet, C through to X (omitting I and O to avoid confusion). The polar regions have their own grid system UPS (Universal Polar Stereographic).

As with the Ordnance Survey grid, you can use the two co-ordinates to give you a numerical reference unique to a particular location on the map. The Easting is always given first followed by the Northing. For example, Scafell Pike is 30 U 0486275E 6034081N (WGS84 datum). Displayed in your gps it will look like this:

30 U 0486275
UTM 6034081

In the UK, places west of Greenwich are in zone 30 U whilst those east of Greenwich are in 31 U. The letters UTM tell you that your gps is in UTM position format and does not form part of the grid reference.

The 30 U tells you the relevant zone: 0486275 is the *Easting* and provides the distance east in metres from the base line of the zone, and 6034081 is the *Northing* and tells you the distance from the equator in metres. On, for example, a 1:50 000 map or 1:25 000 map the grid squares are often one kilometre square and so the co-ordinates can be read off from the map margins. The number of metres within the square both from the Easting and Northing then can be estimated to give you your unique grid reference.

Note: *In the UTM numbering convention Eastings are six digits long and Northings seven digits. Add a 0 to the beginning of the easting when entering it in your gps.*

Entering UTM into your gps

The UTM reference will be entered as: 30 U 0486275 6034081 and displayed on your gps as below:

> **30 U 0486275**
> UTM **6034081** (the UTM tells you your gps is in UTM position format and does not form part of the grid reference)

3 Maps and datums

When you go abroad you will have to work with the maps available. If you have been brought up on Ordnance Survey maps this can be quite an eye opener. *The first thing to do is to check the map to see if there are any grid reference systems and map datums specified.* If you want to look into this before you leave the UK, many maps and further information can be obtained from either the map shop in Upton upon Severn, Gloucestershire, or from branches of Stanfords, or checked on the Internet.

Sales of gps are rising in Europe and many foreign maps are becoming 'gps enabled/compatible', while digital maps are now available in some countries e.g. France, Spain and Germany. Walkers using gps are perhaps best provided for in France. The French equivalent of the Ordnance Survey is the Institut Geographique National (www.ign.fr). Their 'gps compatible' maps in the 1:25 000 Series, which covers France in 350 walking maps, uses the UTM grid (kilometre squares) and datum WGS84. The UTM co-ordinates are printed in blue along the map margins. In Britain (and France), Memory-Map sell digital maps covering the whole

Check foreign maps for grid systems and datums

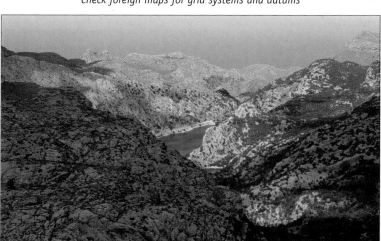

of France using IGN maps. Garmin's French Topo maps for use on Garmin mapping gps and *based* on IGN map data are also available for much of France. Some walkers plan their routes and store them in their gps before going on holiday. Remember walking abroad can be challenging and you need to inform yourself of local factors which might affect your walking, navigation and use of your gps. Your map shop and the internet are good places to start the necessary research.

It must be said that the subject of datums can be very confusing. Around the world there are many datums in use. In the UK we use just one datum OSGB (since 1936) which makes life easier. Many countries have different datums to choose from. Some countries have old and newer datums. *The only sure datum to use is the one specified on the map you want to use.* Remember that your gps reading can be seriously inaccurate by many metres (up to about a kilometre error) when you use a different datum on your gps to that of the map. A number of useful datums to have on your gps for use with European maps is set out below.

Most of Western Europe

WGS84: is becoming more widely used in newer European Maps (GPS enabled/compatible).

European 1950: Austria, Belgium, Denmark, Finland, France, Germany, Gibraltar, Greece, Italy, Luxembourg, Netherlands, Norway, Portugal, Spain, Sweden, Switzerland.

European 1979: Austria, Finland, Netherlands, Norway, Spain, Sweden, Switzerland.

OSGB (GRB36 Magellan): United Kingdom. Ireland 1965: Ireland. Finland Hayford: Finland. Observatorio 1966: Azores. Pico de Las Nieves: Canary Islands. Potsdam: Germany. RT 90: Sweden. CH-1903: Switzerland.

There is a comprehensive list of co-ordinate systems and datums in the 'Help' section of GPSUtility www.gpsu.co.uk (see Help topic on 'datums by country' and 'grids by country'). You can also track down the necessary information on the Internet where you will find a vast amount of information on the subject.

Bibliography

Cliff, P   (2006) Mountain Navigation. A comprehensive
                      concise introduction to the basics of navigation,
                      Cordee. Excellent.

DePriest, D   (2003) GPS User Manual: Working with Garmin
                      Receivers, 1st Books Library. Looks at Garmin gps.

Letham, L   (2003) GPS Made Easy: using the Global
                      Positioning System in the Outdoors, Cordee.
                      Detailed.

McNamara, J   (2004) GPS Navigation for Dummies, Wiley
                      Publishing Inc. Comprehensive.

Peters, J W   (2004) The Complete Idiot's Guide to Geocaching,
                      Penguin-Alpha Books. Good discussion of gps
                      generally.

Useful websites

The Internet is a rich source of information on gps and related matters
and a great number of software programs are available, many of them
free. Websites have links to other websites and you can spend many
hours following up leads on different topics, *if this appeals to you.*
You can manage perfectly well without dipping into this bottomless

It is worth periodically checking your gps manufacturer's websites for updates to your gps software.

Stand-alone PC programs

GPS Utility www.gpsu.co.uk
A popular program originating in the UK. A free, limited version of the software is available that enables you to organise, manage and map gps information.

OZIEXPLORER www.oziexplorer.com
A widely used program: organise, manage and map gps information of Australian origin.

GPS TrackMaker www.gpstm.com
A free program enabling management of gps data and mapping facility.

EasyGPS www.easygps.com

G7ToWin www.gpsinformation.org/ronh

Commercially produced digital maps
www.anquetmaps.com
www.memory-map.co.uk
www.fugawi.com
www.tracklogs.co.uk

Maps on the Internet
www.multimap.com
www.mapblast.com
www.streetmap.co.uk
www.maporama.com/share/
www.maps.yahoo.com
www.ordnancesurvey.co.uk/oswebsite/getamap/

Latitude/longitude and UTM
www.maptools.com/UsingUTM Very helpful on both systems. American.
www.dbartlett.com Dated but still useful. American.
www.colorado.edu/geography/gcraft/notes/coordsys/coordsys_f.html Definitive and detailed. American.
www.dmap.co.uk/utmworld.htm World UTM Grid Zones diagram. Excellent. British.

www.harveymaps.co.uk
Maps produced for walkers at 1:25 000 and 1:40 000 scale.

www.themapshop.co.uk
The Map Shop, 15 High Street, Upton upon Severn, Worcestershire
WR8 0HJ (Tel: 0800 085 40 80).

www.stanfords.co.uk
Stanfords, 12–14 Long Acre, London WC2E 9LP (Tel: 020 7836 1321)
and Bristol (Tel: 0117 929 9966). Maps and related products for the
whole world.

www.ordnancesurvey.co.uk
The Ordnance Survey website contains much useful information on
maps and related topics. (Tel: 08456 050505).

Google Earth
www.earth.google.com
A truly remarkable resource well worth experiencing.

Miscellaneous
www.esa.int
European Space Agency. Updates on the European satellite system.

www.gpsinformation.net
The most informative, authoritative source of information on all
aspects of gps. American.

www.36haroldstreet.freeserve.co.uk
A database of UK hill and mountain waypoints. Also Wainwright
locations.

www.geocaching.com
The best source of information on the treasure hunt using a gps called
geocaching.

www.gagb.org.uk
The website of the Geocaching Association of Great Britain.

www.globalpositioningsystems.co.uk
A reliable, excellent retailer of gps and related products with many
useful links on its website. (Tel: 08453 45 42 45).

www.pocketgps.co.uk
A British website which deals with PDAs and software. There are
articles, reviews and some useful links to other websites.

www.totalwalking.co.uk
The Jarrold website especially for walkers. Includes walk updates for
both the *Pathfinder* and *Short Walks* series, special offers, promotions
and the opportunity to buy online.

www.silva.se
Makers of compasses and all things navigational.

www.ramblers.org.uk
The UK's biggest walking charity.

Memory-Map Navigation Workshop DVD. An interactive introduction
to matters navigational available from Memory-Map and outdoor shops.

Note: *Always check that what you are considering buying is
compatible with your gps receiver or PC.*

Useful addresses for walkers

British Mountaineering Council
177–179 Burton Road, Manchester M20 2BB
Tel: 0870 010 4878
www.thebmc.co.uk
email: office@thebmc.co.uk
Promotes the interests of climbers, hillwalkers and mountaineers.

British Orienteering Federation
8a Stancliffe House, Whitworth Road, Darley Dale, Matlock DE4 2HJ
Tel: 01629 734042
www.britishorienteering.org.uk
email: bof@britishorienteering.org.uk
*An entertaining way to hone your navigation skills. They do not use
gps because orienteering maps do not use grid references.*

Harvey Map Services Ltd
12–22 Main Street, Doune, Perthshire FK16 6BJ
Tel: 01786 841202
www.harveymaps.co.uk
email: sales@harveymaps.co.uk

Ordnance Survey
Romsey Road, Maybush,
Southampton SO16 4GU
Tel: 08456 050505
www.ordnancesurvey.co.uk
email: customerservices@ordnancesurvey.co.uk

Ramblers' Association
Main Office, 2nd Floor, Camelford House,
87–90 Albert Embankment,
London SE1 7TW
Tel: 020 7339 8500
www.ramblers.org.uk
email: ramblers@london.ramblers.org.uk
A mine of information on all aspects of walking.

Ramblers Holidays
Lemsford Mill, Lemsford Village,
Welwyn Garden City, AL8 7TR
Tel: 01707 331133
www.ramblersholidays.co.uk
email: info@ramblersholidays.co.uk
Organises walking holidays in the UK and all over the world.

Royal Society for the Protection of Birds
UK Headquarters, The Lodge, Sandy,
Bedfordshire SG19 2DL
Tel: 01767 680551
www.rspb.org.uk

The National Trust
PO Box 39,
Warrington WA5 7WD
Tel: 0870 458 4000
www.nationaltrust.org.uk
email: enquiries@thenationaltrust.org.uk

YHA National Office
Trevelyan House, Dimple Road, Matlock,
Derbyshire DE4 3YH
Tel: 01629 592600
www.yha.org.uk
email: customerservices@yha.org.uk

Acknowledgements

In writing this book I have received a great deal of help and encouragement. Alan Murphy's advice and expertise so generously given have been invaluable. He is the author of GPS Utility. I would also like to thank Graham Hughes of Anquet Technology Ltd for his help and support; Shelley Grimwood, Managing Editor of Jarrold Publishing, for being such a positive force; Richard Thomas-Martinez for his unfailing encouragement; and, for her valuable editorial input, Elizabeth Walsh, partner, friend and walking companion, to whom this book is dedicated.

Picture credits